Divorce Mediation

John M. Haynes, Ph.D., is an Associate Professor at the School of Social Welfare, State University of New York at Stony Brook, where he teaches social policy and mediation.

In addition to his private practice as a divorce mediator, he directs the Divorce Mediation Project of the Family Service Association of Nassau County. He runs workshops and seminars for training mediators.

Dr. Haynes serves on the Board of Directors of the Family Mediation Association, a national organization of divorce mediators. He is the Deputy Editor of the *Journal of the Society for the Study of Symbolic Interaction* and a book reviewer for *Library Journal*.

The author came to academia from the labor movement, where he first learned the art of negotiating and mediating. During those years he was a special assistant to the President of the International Union of Electrical, Radio and Machine Workers, AFL-CIO, and a speechwriter for numerous public officials.

He is a member of the Association of Family Conciliation Courts and the National Association of Social Workers. He is married, has two teenage daughters, and resides in Northport on Long Island, New York.

John M. Haynes, Ph.D.

Divorce Mediation

A practical guide for therapists and counselors

Springer Publishing Company
New York

306.89
H424d

Springer Publishing Company, Inc.
200 Park Avenue South
New York, New York 10003

82 83 84 85 / 10 9 8 7 6 5 4 3

Library of Congress Cataloging in Publication Data

Haynes, John M
    Divorce mediation.

    Bibliography: p.
    Includes index.
    1. Divorce mediation—United States. 2. Divorce
mediation—United States—Case studies. I. Title.
[DNLM: 1. Divorce. 2. Counseling. WM 55 H424d]
HQ834.H39   306.8'9   80-25065
ISBN 0-8261-2590-5
ISBN 0-8261-2591-3 (pbk.)

Printed in the United States of America

*To Gretchen
with whom nothing is impossible*

Contents

Acknowledgments

Many individuals over the years have supported, encouraged, and influenced my work in the field of divorce mediation. Unfortunately, I am unable to detail each person's contribution. I would, however, like to express sincere appreciation and gratitude to my mentor Sandy Kravitz, Edee Harshbarger, Ed Wingard, Sal Ambrosino, Virginia Zaremba, David Kadane, John and Susan Garret, and Jean Tracy. I am indebted to my colleagues at the Family Studies Center: Stanley Seigel, Bob Polin, and Winnie Jolly for their generous offers of assistance and advice. I am also grateful for the support of my associates at the School of Social Welfare, particularly Robert Lefferts, a trusted and trusting friend who is a continual source of encouragement to me. Above all, a warm thank you must go to my wife, Gretchen, and to our daughters, Karen and Julia. Their gift to me of time, space, and love made this book possible.

Introduction

Divorce is rapidly becoming the norm. As Glick and Norton point out, approximately 40 percent of the marriages of women in their late twenties will end in divorce (1977, p. 18). The majority of those divorces will be handled by attorneys, involving the couples in the traditional adversarial legal system. In the process the couples will experience great frustration that will add to the anger and pain already present in the marriage dissolution. The nature of the legal system removes a great deal of power from the couple. Thus, one of the most important events in their lives, the dissolution of the marriage, takes place in large part outside of their control.

This book proposes an alternative way of dissolving the marriage: divorce mediation. I seek to establish that people can be empowered to negotiate their own divorce settlement outside of the legal system and in a nonadversarial way. The model of divorce mediation is drawn from my experiences in labor mediation. My experience as a social work educator, furthermore, enables me to integrate the professional and labor knowledge into a new model of divorce mediation as presented in Chapter 1.

In implementing the model I make certain assumptions. First, the mediator must have a clear understanding of the overall divorce adjustment process and how divorce mediation fits into the total experience. Chapter 2 presents a theory of divorce and the adjustment process couples must go through, moving from a marriage to two separate lives. The second assumption, based on this theoretical framework, is that divorce mediation can, by reducing the pain and focusing the couple on the tasks of negotiating, reduce the turbulence experienced by the family during the dissolution. The third assumption is that if divorce mediation is successful, it will not only help the couple to negotiate their own agreement but will also help them to adjust to the divorce more quickly than if they had used the adversarial process.

Children in divorcing families probably carry the heaviest burden of the divorce. The model and methodology suggest ways in which the children can be involved in the mediation process. Chapter 3 discusses some of the problems encountered by children and how these problems are dealt with in most divorcing families.

The model is discussed in Chapters 4 and 5. Chapter 4 examines the referral system and its impact on mediation and shows how divorce mediation can be added to most clinicians' current practice. This chapter also examines the blockages that occur when couples are not ready to divorce and the power relationship within the marriage that shapes the mediation. Chapter 5 lays out the step-by-step process of negotiating and also examines which factors lead to a successful agreement and which inhibit an agreement.

The case studies in Chapter 6 demonstrate several situations in which mediation worked and a few in which it did not. This chapter will also help the reader determine how best to integrate mediation into his/her practice. The ethical issues that emerge from mediation are discussed in Chapter 7, along with suggestions for starting a professional practice, including addresses of relevant sources.

Appendix A is a manual which I have developed to give to clients entering divorce mediation. Its purpose is to help clients understand the process and to demystify it. I believe it describes the methods and the process of divorce mediation clearly and will add to the reader's understanding of the material in the earlier chapters. Appendix B consists of sample separation agreements, demonstrating the range of issues covered in divorce mediation. The reader is able to see how the negotiating process of preparation, goal setting, and bargaining is finally rendered into written form.

Divorce mediation breaks new ground. It opens the possibility of a new field of professional practice and a way of expanding the parameters of current practice. It also suggests an alternative way of using family courts. There is a great deal of discussion in family agencies, the courts, and among professional therapists about how to help families engaged in a divorce.

When working with families the therapist is often faced with the possibility that a trial or temporary separation would help the couple examine the marriage from a new perspective. Suggesting a temporary separation as a therapeutic strategy requires that the couple be able to reach an agreement on the terms of the separation. The material in this book can and should be used by therapists to facilitate the arrangement of a separation so as to be able to make the most therapeutically productive use of the period of separation.

One note about style. I have chosen to use the s/he designation in an attempt to avoid the constant sexist use of the masculine form. I have also used "couple" as a plural, partly to ease the problem of sexism in language and partly in recognition that there are two to a couple, each with her/his own identity.

Divorce Mediation

part I

Professional intervention in divorce situations

chapter 1

Divorce mediation:
an expansion
of clinical practice

The pain, anger, and frustration of divorce are frequently exacerbated by the legal process as it presently works. Often the helping professional who has been involved with the family during the period leading up to the decision to divorce is excluded from the proceedings, and the clients are referred to another profession. However, it is precisely at this time that the special skills of the therapist-counselor are most needed. This chapter proposes an expansion of clinical practice to include divorce mediation. Although divorce laws differ from state to state, the role of a divorce mediator as described here is relevant to all the states of the union.

Forty-seven states have a form of "no fault" divorce, which does not require either party to prove fault on the part of the spouse. Rather, the divorce may be obtained on the following grounds:

1. irretrievably broken marriage,
2. irreconcilable differences,
3. incompatibility.

The actual divorce is preceded by a legal separation period of six to twenty-four months. The couple live apart for the stipulated period on the basis of a mutual understanding that a continued marriage is impossible. Although the laws provide for the couple to enter into a separation agreement that can be converted to a permanent divorce agreement at the end of the mandated separation period, it is not a requirement. A mediated settlement lays the groundwork for a more amicable and therefore more personally productive separation. This, in turn, reduces the turbulence surrounding the divorce itself and shortens the period of adjustment experienced by all divorcing couples.

In undertaking the role of divorce mediator, the helping professional must first overcome the reluctance of being party to a family's breakup.

3

Most therapists see their role as a supportive one and use their professional skills in assisting families to resolve their problems and stay together. However, there are times when no amount of intervention can hold a marriage together. In this context the family therapist has a special responsibility to develop mediation skills. The family or couple therapist helps the couple to identify what is wrong with the relationship/marriage and then assists them or the family in taking corrective action. However, in some cases this search will lead to the jointly held conclusion that the appropriate action is divorce. Once this decision has been reached, the therapist has an ethical responsibility to complete the uncoupling process. Divorce mediation is the most efficient way of accomplishing this.

Once divorce is inevitable, the professional's role changes to one of attempting to make the separation as painless as possible, to help the couple maintain their individual dignity, and to assist the children to make the transition by reducing the conflict inherent in the process of divorce. The decision to separate is not the beginning of a new process; rather it is a point on the continuum of a dissolving marriage. The events leading up to the decision to end the marriage play an important part in the divorce process. The therapist who has been helping the couple up to this point is better informed about the total picture than a lawyer would be and more able to use this knowledge to facilitate the divorce.

But even if the couple has not previously been in therapy, the professional helper is still more qualified to help dissolve the marriage because, by virtue of the special training, s/he can elicit the causes for the end of the marriage and use that knowledge to help make the divorce process a productive turning point in the couple's lives.

It is the therapist, therefore, who offers a divorcing couple the best set of specialist skills to implement their decision. If there has been previous therapy, the therapist–couple relationship is maintained and used to facilitate the divorce. If, however, this relationship interferes with the mediation role, another therapist can work with the couple and, using the same therapeutic skills, facilitate their decision to divorce. Or, if the couple have not tried therapy, a therapist can first ascertain whether marriage counseling will help them hold the marriage together and, in the event that the marriage relationship is past the point of no return, use her/his skills to aid in the divorce process.

In addition many couples are using the "no fault" process to enter into trial separations. They hope to be able to work things out more effectively if they are not in daily contact. At times this form of separation is recommended by the therapist as a way of relieving some of the pressures building up in the relationship.

The problem is that it becomes increasingly necessary for the couple to have a formal agreement covering their respective interests during the trial separation. If they go to lawyers to do this, the lawyers' training is likely to make them adversaries and then the act of developing a trial separation agreement becomes a focus for increasing hostilities, which makes reconciliation less likely. A trial separation agreement drafted with the aid of a divorce mediator, however, who is also seeing the couple in therapy, is more likely to reduce the anger and struggle about the content of the agreement and create an atmosphere of cooperation, which enhances the chances of reconciliation.

At present, when a couple decides to divorce, each party goes to an attorney who is trained in the adversary role. The two attorneys then represent one client against the other. Much of the decision making is taken out of the hands of the clients, as the attorneys engage in battle within the legal system. This process serves to feed the destructiveness and anger already present in the dissolving relationship.

Lawyers represent their clients to the best of their abilities, regardless of the possible effect on the other party. Thus, they tend to push their particular client to win every possible advantage. This tactic provides the couple with another arena in which to battle out the issues that led to the divorce, at the same time that they are trying to negotiate a settlement. The adversary process of settling the financial aspects of the separation can only worsen the already deteriorating social relationship. In an American Bar Association survey of judges, friends of the court, and commissioners of domestic relations, 89 percent of the respondents cited financial problems as one of the major causes of divorce (Nuccio, 1967, p. 2).

While the legal process emphasizes a win–lose outcome, with each party striving to be the winner, mediation emphasizes a win–win outcome, with each partner emerging from the negotiations with positive gains, while recognizing the right and need of the other also to have gains. Thus the mediator carefully focuses the couple on ways of achieving their individual goals that make it possible for the other also to achieve goals. This focus demands cooperation rather than competition and the cooperation is orchestrated by the mediator.

Deutsch has demonstrated that the cooperative approach enhances open and honest communication and helps get the relevant facts onto the table. It encourages the recognition of the legitimacy of the other's interests and stimulates the perception of the other's benevolence (1973, p. 363). By concentrating on the cooperative approach, divorce mediation helps establish a new relationship between the couple, one that is productive in the negotiations and in their future, as they continue to deal with each other as regards their children. In developing a win–win outcome, the mediator prevents victories for one partner by making sure that for each concession, or "win," enjoyed by one, there is an equal concession, or "win," for the other. Ideally, the "win" for each party is contained within the same issue. Almost all differences between people can be mediated to assure some sharing in a positive outcome.

The economics of divorce

When the real economic factors of divorce are understood, there is little room for maneuvering. Assume that a couple with a two-year-old child lives in New York City. Such a family needs $10,785 after taxes in order to maintain a moderate standard of living (Community Council of Greater New York, 1976a). When the household breaks up, the total need rises to $13,489 to maintain the same level for the two households. Thus the way in which a division can be made is restricted from the start.

The husband and wife will now be filing individual tax returns. The husband will pay about $3,000 in Social Security and income taxes on his original wages, and the wife is taxed on whatever income she receives in alimony. The increased tax liability of an average alimony raises the joint tax liability to $3,517. Thus if the two households are to be maintained at the predivorce standard of living, there is not only little money to divide, but there may also be an actual need to increase the income by means of a second job (Community Council of Greater New York, 1976b). Therefore, unless the couple had been living at a lower standard than their income allowed, there is little room for economic maneuvering. The other economic assets in a marriage—the home, furnishings, car, or the like—must be divided as well. However, the real needs of both the husband and wife again impose a narrow range of choices.

The battle between the attorneys usually takes place outside the courtroom as they attempt to divide the property by agreement. However, the adversarial precept "to represent my client to the best of my abilities" does not help resolve the emotional aspects of divorce. Not only is the attorney untrained in the area of interpersonal relationships, but the Canons of Judicial and Professional Ethics issued by the American Bar Association state:

> The professional judgement of a lawyer should be exercised, within the bounds of the law, solely for the benefit of his client and free of compromising influences and other loyalties. Neither his personal interests, the interests of other clients, nor the desires of third persons should be permitted to dilute his loyalty to his client [McKinney, 1975, p. 438].

This position is certainly not supportive of the give-and-take compromise that is essential for a mature divorce settlement.   ·

If the attorneys cannot agree on an out-of-court settlement, the matter goes before a judge. The judge is confined by the same set of facts that the attorneys are, and the court's decision will generally reflect what is considered possible. Moreover, neither husband nor wife has any real effect on the outcome. This lack of involvement leaves both parties aggrieved and angry at the court and at the attorneys, and even more antagonistic toward one another. There are no winners in this war.

Many of the emotional hurts and feelings of guilt involved in divorce are displayed during the struggle for an economic settlement. The attorney is neither equipped to deal with a client's emotional upheaval, nor is s/he interested. S/he is looking for a settlement that can be taken into court for approval. Thus when a couple attempt to settle the emotional issues of the separation by engaging in economic war, neither partner can win. Even if there were room for compromise, money cannot resolve the emotional damage of marital breakup. It is at this point that intervention on the part of the therapist or counselor can be helpful. S/he can understand how damaging this settlement process is to the parties as individuals and work toward an emotional as well as economic settlement.

Will lawyers oppose this expansion of clinical practice? Obviously, some will. The main opposition will come from those attorneys who derive most of their income from a divorce practice. However, most lawyers do not engage in divorce cases exclusively and do not like to handle such cases. Many lawyers recognize the limitations of their training and prefer not to have to deal with the heavy emotional issues inherently part of any divorce. They would and do prefer to have the therapist handle the negotiations leading up to the drafting of the separation agreement. In those cases the lawyer acts more as a consultant, checking the agreement drawn up by the clients and the mediator-therapist for legal accuracy and appropriateness, and assuring the clients that they are accomplishing in the written document the goals they sought in the negotiations. They then incorporate the negotiated draft into the full, legal separation agreement.

Labor mediation

The concept of a divorce mediator advanced in this book is modeled on that of a labor mediator. In a labor strike the government frequently sends in a mediator to assist the parties in reaching a settlement—and that is the only function the mediator has. S/he has no attachment or allegiance either to management or to labor and should be careful not to become identified with either party.

The labor mediator begins by meeting with each side separately and concentrating on the primary issues on which both parties have reached an agreement. These are put into writing and removed from the bargaining arena. S/he then attempts to identify the symbolic issues that have been raised, but which neither side seriously expects to resolve. For example, in negotiations with a nationwide corporation, a union demanded a union-shop clause that would require all employees to join the union as a condition of employment. The company, however, was well known to be unalterably opposed to such a measure. The mediator had to determine how strongly the union felt on this issue—whether it was a real issue to be resolved at the bargaining table or a symbolic one that had been raised by the union to win its members' support.

The mediator slowly winnows the agreed-upon points from the symbolic issues until the substantial issues of disagreement are identified and the real bargaining can begin. Sometimes s/he meets privately with each party or, if s/he thinks there is a chance for mutual agreement on a new item, will bring both parties together at the table. When the mediator meets with each party privately, s/he probes to determine what is possible. Frequently, one party uses the mediator to try out ideas that would be too risky to confront the other party with directly. The mediator then attempts to show each side what substantial areas of disagreement need to be resolved before a settlement can be reached. The final compromise is made by the two parties, based on their assessment of their individual needs.

The labor mediator is paid by the government. Her/his function is to reach a settlement, and because s/he is trusted by both parties, s/he is able to accomplish this. S/he does not represent either side but represents a settlement that both sides can accept. How can this experience be applied to the helping professional in her/his new role as divorce mediator? Once the decision to divorce has been made, the parties can jointly hire the mediator. By sharing the payment each shares the responsibility and the control, and neither is beholden to the other for the service.

Preparing for negotiation

In the role of the divorce mediator, the professional—as mentioned before—assists the parties to reach a fair settlement in a way that enables them to separate the economic issues from the emotional ones. In the process, s/he performs the function of helping the clients focus on the future rather than the past. However, the mediator maintains the original therapeutic or counseling function as well. At this critical moment, s/he may be the only person in the couple's lives who is nonjudgmental and interested solely in their needs.

Later chapters will demonstrate the negotiation process step by step, drawing on case histories to illustrate various points. Here I will offer the broad-brush design, using the term *mediator* to denote when the professional assumes that role and *therapist* to denote the times when the professional primarily fills that function.

The professional must decide at what point the couple cannot be reconciled and divorce mediation becomes appropriate. Chapter 2 discusses the various stages of predivorce emotional states and helps locate the individuals along a continuum of divorce proceedings. Timing can be crucial. As I will demonstrate, a premature move toward divorce can be frustrated by the reluctant party and mediation will bog down. This situation will be dealt with in detail in Chapters 5 and 6.

Now let us assume that the couple are ready to begin the mediation process. To ascertain how the division can take place, the divorce mediator first meets with each party separately. This is an important step, because initially the two sides will probably disagree about the future earning ability of each party separately.

If the wife is not earning an income at this time, the mediator assists the parties to arrive at a projection of what the husband's future income will be. This allows the couple, but particularly the wife, to begin thinking about their future independence. Each person is then asked to draft a list of what family expenses they have had during the past year and to plan an estimated budget to cover their new lives apart. This helps both husband and wife to define one another's needs realistically. In order to complete the picture and obtain a sound indication of what each side believes he or she needs, the mediator also asks the couple to develop a statement of the net worth of each partner.

Once the economic data base has been agreed upon, the mediator attempts to define those sentimental or emotional items that may be critical to a settlement. For example, the record collection may be extremely important to one party, and the mediator must be aware of this. During this time the continuing emotional issues concerning the separation will begin to surface. "I don't want him visiting the kids too much and influencing them." "I don't want her to have men friends in the house." Such views are commonly expressed, and the therapist identifies and catalogs them, using her/his skills to help each party deal with them.

It is important that the divorce mediator clearly establish that s/he is not representing either party but is interested only in achieving a settlement. However, the settlement involves both economic and emotional issues. At the same time that the mediator helps settle the economic divisions, s/he also helps the couple to place the marriage behind them, to deal with the emotional issues that caused the divorce, and to look forward to the future.

Many divorce settlements take years to reach because both parties in turn take advantage of the settlement process to put off the final act of dissolution. On the one hand, the issues causing the separation are too great to permit the marriage to continue. On the other hand, the husband or wife may continue to cling to the unsuccessful marriage, because the problems have not been resolved in a way that permits the parties to move forward. Clearly, this is unhealthy for the couple and devastating for the children.

When people cling to their partners because of unresolved issues concerning the separation, the professional must draw on her/his therapeutic skills to help them work through these problems. This helps to avoid the danger that conflicts remain unresolved even after the divorce is final. Unfortunately a large number of people return to court time after time for years after the decree is granted. When the emotional blocks are severe and seriously impede the couple's work on the separation, the mediator calls for a "time-out" from the mediation for a specified number of sessions. I usually ask for a three-session time-out and the couple understand that during that time my role will switch from mediator to therapist and the focus of the session will be on an examination of feelings rather than on problem solving. Once the couple has been helped by the mediator-therapist to overcome their resistance to dealing with the emotional problems, they can begin to focus on the economic issues.

Negotiating a settlement

Eventually the mediator will have reached an agreed-upon data base and will have a broad idea of how the existing assets and future earnings of a couple can be divided. Having ascertained the boundaries for a settlement, s/he can identify the areas of common agreement. S/he proceeds, as a labor mediator might, to reduce those items to a rough memo form so that they can be removed from the discussion. In addition, the mediator identifies those demands that are advanced to satisfy an emotional need and those used by either party as a strategy. This permits the mediator to remove the areas of agreement from consideration and to isolate the symbolic issues, thus leaving only the substantive issues of disagreement. These substantive issues can then be measured against the budgetary figures at which the mediator and couple arrived together during the assessment period. The mediator will present these figures, along with the current cost-of-living budgets from the Bureau of Labor Statistics, at the time that s/he determines the information can be most advantageously used to arrive at a settlement.

At this point most couples will begin to grasp fully the financial implications of divorce (Porter, 1975). For both parties it will mean not only profound emotional changes but a significant drop in their standard of living. The mediator helps some couples face the fact that divorce may mean living at the poverty level (Crittenden, 1977, p. 26). As they understand the reality of the situation, the chances of either party blaming herself or himself or the spouse for the new financial situation are diminished.

As the mediator shuttles between the two parties, s/he creates an atmosphere of trust that permits either party to try out an idea without losing face. For example, s/he has learned that one party feels strongly about the record collection. The other party knows this fact and might try to use it as a weapon. The mediator, however, can help the second party to consider the possibility of trading the book collection for the records. The mediator then broaches that idea to the first party and, if an agreement is reached, brings the two together to strike another "deal." As the man and woman begin to come to terms with the situation, their mutual respect is restored. With the assistance of the professional the couple can begin to deal with the emotional issues directly, thus reducing the need to use economic issues for emotional ends. Once this begins, a settlement becomes possible—one that each feels is fair and that each can live with. Most important, it leaves both parties with their individual dignity intact. The positive effect of this process is also felt by the children, who are removed from the damaging position of being bargaining tools.

Throughout the bargaining process the professional makes a unique contribution. Therapeutic or counseling training teaches her/him to be self-aware, empathic to the clients, and understanding of past issues that may never have been resolved. By creating a therapeutic atmosphere, therefore, s/he can assist the clients to identify personal blocks and internal problems.

Helping the client
face the future

During the mediation period the couple is helped to let go of the past and begin to focus on the future. By defining the conflict between the two partners explicitly at the point of separation, the professional helps the family to resolve it and to work toward their new relationship. Throughout, the professional neutralizes the situation, preventing any exacerbation of already existing tension. In assisting the parties to reach a settlement, s/he defuses the anger, focuses the rage, and turns the couple from the past to the future.

The concept of mediation is implicit in the role of therapist-counselor. Not only because of their professional ethics but also because of their training and experience all such professionals—but particularly those specializing in family therapy—are uniquely qualified to perform the task of mediation. In labor negotiations there is a tendency for the mediator to expect the weaker of the two parties to give up the most. However, in divorce mediations any identification with one side immediately destroys the mediator's effectiveness. Although the mediator realizes that both sides will be susceptible to different external pressures, s/he uses this difference productively in the search for a fair agreement.

Because of the historical sexism in this society, the wife is more likely to be vulnerable to pressures from the uncertainties of life that force her to bring up the children without her previous source of steady income and companionship. The professional must try to keep these fears from causing the woman to attempt to reach an early settlement that would not necessarily be in her long-term best interest. Alternatively, if the husband manifests considerable guilt about walking away from his family, the professional must not permit him to assuage his feelings by making an unrealistic settlement that he cannot maintain.

The professional is often faced with unresolved forms of destructive behavior that have been built into the marital relationship. If mediation is to provide the couple with the atmosphere in which to reach a self-determined settlement, additional information must be given to both husband and wife. According to the National Organization for Women, in over 50 percent of all alimony cases "the man falls behind on payments within two years, often intentionally" (Vecsey, 1977, p. 26). This may be because he feels the settlement was imposed on him from the outside, and he therefore becomes increasingly unhappy with it. As time passes, anger that was not resolved at the time of the divorce increases to the point at which the husband feels justified in stopping payments. The courts are notoriously slow in enforcing divorce settlements, and women frequently find the agreement to be valueless. These factors should be considered at the time of the divorce. The woman should know what the odds are of receiving alimony payments past the two-year period.

This raises another issue. Should a settlement be attempted that does not have as a goal the liberation of the woman from her dependence on the income-producing man? The legislatures are changing divorce laws in many states, providing for equal distribution of property and a time-defined "rehabilitative" alimony. Unless this form of alimony is accompanied by a thoughtful plan, the woman could run through the alimony period without gaining her needed independence.

As I have emphasized, the mediator should attempt to focus the couple's attention on the years to come. This could involve a two-step settlement. At first, alimony payments could be high enough to allow the woman to obtain further training or education. Following this period, alimony could be phased out. The woman would become self-supporting, leaving the man responsible only for his share of child support. Such a plan, tailored to the specific needs of the couple, gives them a realizable goal. For the woman it is financial independence from the man. For the man it is financial independence from alimony payments within an agreed-upon period of time. Furthermore, in all likelihood such an agreement, reached maturely by both parties, would be honored more fully than an open-ended one imposed from the outside. There are further advantages to the use of a divorce mediator instead of a lawyer, both to the judiciary and to the couple. For the judiciary the process alleviates overburdened court schedules. Although attorneys continue to be responsible for reviewing the final agreement and obtaining the court decrees, they are freed from dealing with the couple's emotional conflicts, a situation for which they are not trained. Because the fee of the divorce mediator is usually lower than that of an attorney, the cost to the couple of using a mediator is considerably less. The benefits derived from the mediator's service, however, are greater than those from the attorney's, because mediation focuses on a solution, not a win–lose struggle. Thus the couple receive assistance in going through a painful and emotionally searing experience, at the same time that they maintain a sense of control over their own lives.

Conclusion

The process of therapeutic divorce mediation offers the couple a setting in which they can reach a joint settlement that will be beneficial to both. In presenting her/himself as a friend of both parties, and not as an arbiter, the mediator might say: "I cannot define the settlement and I cannot impose an agreement upon you. My role is to assist you in reaching your agreement. I will not take sides on any of the issues. I am interested in the settlement as a principle, and I am interested in you as people. I feel for your pain and want to help you through this difficult process and help diminish this pain. Finally, I hope to help you use these negotiations to place the past behind you. The marriage is ending but you have a life ahead of you. That new life can be marred by holding onto the anger of the separation. Or the new life can be an exciting opportunity to "redefine yourself."

Thus the mediator turns the couple's focus away from past anger and recriminations. By being nonjudgmental s/he works with the couple so that they reach a settlement that permits them both to concentrate on the future and the potential it holds.

chapter 2

The emotional aspects
of divorce

Divorce mediation takes place during a period of emotional turmoil for the couple. Many changes occur in both parties and the emotional response to the act of divorce has a significant impact on the behavior of the participants. Thus when a couple arrive at divorce mediation, it is important for the mediator to understand the broader emotional context in which they function. A considerable number of studies has been completed (Hetherington, Cox, & Cox, 1976; Kessler, 1975; Laner, 1976; Weiss, 1975) on the impact of divorce, and a coherent theoretical framework has been developed, which is helpful to the professional. We shall call this the Divorce Adjustment Process.

In looking at the Divorce Adjustment Process we shall examine the way in which it affects mediation. We shall also examine the therapeutic role of the professional in working with clients. We shall place divorce mediation within this process and demonstrate how the professional can assist in a more rapid and satisfactory adjustment to divorce. We will identify the two different roles the professional must assume: therapist and mediator.

In the beginning of the divorce process much of the intervention will continue the professional's therapeutic function. As mediation increases, different strategies are called for and the professional must recognize which strategy is appropriate so that s/he can be most effective. During the actual negotiations the mediator will need to assume the therapeutic role when it assists mediation. If, during mediation, the professional finds that therapy is the primary role, this would indicate either that the couple may not be ready for divorce or that they are moving toward the divorce too quickly. By understanding the Divorce Adjustment Process the professional is able to determine when each role—therapist or mediator—is most appropriate.

The Divorce Adjustment Process, as described by Joseph Federico of the Divorce Adjustment Institute in Chicago, includes four basic developmental stages: deliberation, litigation, transition, and redirection. These stages are not chronologically coherent. Clients can be in more than one developmental stage at the same time. The divorce mediation period includes the litigation stage and the transition stage. In certain cases the couple may still be in the deliberation stage; it is important for the professional to be able to determine just which stage is being experienced by the couple if s/he is to be most helpful in negotiating the separation agreement.

Following the discussion of the four developmental stages of divorce, we will examine the way in which the clients' feelings and behavior in response to the divorce affect their ability to mediate their differences. If the professional understands these feelings and can locate the behavior in the Divorce Adjustment Process, s/he will also know which of those factors are transitory and which are long-term needs that must be included in the final separation agreement.

The divorce adjustment process

Deliberation

This is the period between the time the idea of divorce is first raised and the implementation of the idea. The significance of this period is rarely understood by either party at the time although, in retrospect, many people can recall the moment they decided that the possibility of divorce became real—a point that can be described as the marital point of no return (Federico, 1979, p. 95). From that moment onward, the party making the decision begins to gear up for the ultimate action.

The indicators of this period are rarely verbal. However, there are usually clear behavioral indicators, such as short pay checks, an affair, ceasing to provide services to the partner, or, in the extreme, physical abuse. It can be determined from these actions that the person wants to harm the relationship. The therapist in this period would therefore want to reflect back the behavior as well as the articulated feelings of the client. It is rare that both partners reach this point of no return at the same time. Because it is only vaguely understood, the initiator is often reluctant to articulate the desire. Thus the therapist would make it her/his goal to assist the initiator in acknowledging the desire and telling it to the partner so that it can be dealt with. At this point there is still a high chance of getting the problems on the table to permit the couple to deal with them in a way that assists them to continue the marriage.

Kessler suggests that among the sources of imbalance in a marriage that often lead to divorce is a lack of conflict resolution skills (1975, p. 60). Since divorce mediation leans heavily on effective conflict resolution, its use could either prove difficult for many clients or become the means for learning new skills to restructure the marriage. It is likely that the couple, at the point at which they seek divorce mediation, are too heavily invested in specific behavior to be able to use the conflict resolution skills for anything except to separate. However, the skills can be learned and used in future relationships.

The initiating party often chooses one of two strategies to shift the cause for the divorce onto the spouse.

1. *Provocation.* The initiator attempts to force the other partner to seek the divorce (Federico, 1979, p. 100). This is done through a series of escalating actions aimed at disrupting the marriage, in anticipation that at some point the other party will seek a divorce in sheer exasperation. This would explain the often-heard complaint, "I've filed for divorce, got almost everything I wanted, but I'm still unhappy." These escalating actions could also be a cry for help from the initiating partner, indicating a desire for changes in the marriage relationship (Bohannan, 1970, p. 40).

The professional needs to know the process by which the couple arrived at the decision to divorce because, if the filing partner is not in fact the initiator but is merely reacting to provocation, s/he would be propelled by a different set of desires in the negotiations. Indeed, if either partner had been trapped into seeking an unwanted divorce, the professional could expect considerable resistance in the negotiations. It would also help to understand the provoker's role, since it may well be played out in the negotiations in an overeagerness to reach a settlement, perhaps to the long-term detriment of both parties.

2. *Sabotage.* The second method used by the initiator to avoid apparent responsibility for the actual divorce action is described as sabotage. Here the initiator provokes the noninitiator; the spouse, however, is resilient and accepts the provoking behavior. Thus the actions are escalated until the spouse begins to retaliate by his/her own hurtful behavior. Then the initiator is able to say, "I want out," based on the actions of the other person. The noninitiator is blamed for the ultimate decision to divorce (Federico, 1979, p. 103).

In this way the rejecting spouse suggests that it is the rejected individual's own fault that he or she was abandoned (Weiss, 1975, p. 100). Virginia Satir has pointed out that rejection is made up of two parts, a "no" plus "you are no damn good" (Satir et al., 1975, p. 151).

The task of the therapist during this period would be to identify any sabotage behavior. In the process s/he can determine how destructive the actions are and how invested the initiator is in following them through to a divorce. It has been shown that displeasurable aspects of marriage are independent of, and more important than, the pleasurable aspects (Thomas, 1977, p. 16). Therefore, the therapist would want to concentrate on reducing the behavior of the spouse that was displeasurable rather than focus on the pleasurable behavior.

Litigation

This is the second period in the Divorce Adjustment Process. It usually runs about one year, defined as it is by the legal requirements. For example, in some states a couple can separate and file a separation agreement that becomes the divorce settlement one year later. In other states the waiting period is six months.

The first call to the lawyer is often a bluff to the other partner; it is a weapon with which to seek change in the relationship. Apparently, divorce lawyers see about 50 percent of their clients only once or twice, and then receive a phone call that the marriage is straightening out. However, when the action is deliberately taken and divorce proceedings begin, partners cannot continue to act in the same way as they did in the past. They are now moving toward dissolution and the past relationships cannot be maintained.

This can be a most productive period in helping the client to change roles in relation to the partner. The therapist can use the legal struggle to indicate how things are changing and to point out that unless the client begins to redefine his/her role, the post-divorce period will merely replicate the marriage relationships. Therefore, the therapist needs to help the couple begin to define a new relationship between themselves. This is the central therapeutic function during the period of the Divorce Adjustment Process. It is also important at this point to help the children understand the redefined roles as they are taking shape.

If the mediator understands that the litigation period begins the redefinition of roles (indeed, it must do so if the people involved are to come out of the process in a positive way), s/he can help the couple extract an even greater learning experience from the litigation process by their being involved in and having control over the legal proceedings. This control speaks to the central point of the model I have developed—empowerment of the couple. Rather than artificially excluding the litigative actions from the Divorce Adjustment Process, the mediator integrates the negotiations into the therapeutic process by helping both parties redefine their relationship and roles through their active participation and control over the marriage dissolution. Thus mediation adds an important element of self-control to the Divorce Adjustment Process, which enhances the total learning and growth that is possible from this painful experience.

The "friendly divorce" can provide the couple with a means of assuring themselves that the total marriage was not a waste. By reducing the turbulence, the partners can help each other deal with the frustration and fearfulness most people experience in divorce (Weiss, 1975, p. 67).

Transition

This period includes a time of "nuttiness." It is a period of irrational behavior when clients often indicate a knowledge that what they are doing is irrational as well as a feeling that they have no control over these actions. It can be described as a period of feeling pressured, of panic behavior. Therefore they need reassurance that this behavior is okay, that they are not losing their minds, that this is a normal part of the process. The stress reaction is caused by being confronted with the fact of being alone; there is no companionship and no sense of security—things that people often actually married for.

The therapist must observe these symptoms, ask, "Why this one?" and then take a literal approach to understanding them. For example, hyperventilation can indicate that something in the client's life is suffocating him/her. If constant vomiting is the problem, something in that person's life is making him/her sick. It is unlikely that the client is going to be able to deal with the cause of these symptoms at that moment, but its identification by the therapist can be filed away for later use when the client is able to deal with it.

The therapist can expect a high degree of frustration as the client takes one step forward and two steps back. The transition period is rarely developmentally stable. This has implications for the mediator. During this period, the therapist needs to repeat ideas frequently. Stress interferes with the client's ability to focus, and ideas therefore will rarely be grasped the first time they are raised. Since the litigation and transition periods overlap, the mediator must expect to repeat constantly the ideas developed in the negotiations.

The transition period follows the physical separation. The therapist's goals during this period should be to assist the parties in developing an emotional divorce. That is, up until this period the emphasis has been on the physical separation. However, once that is attained, there is still the problem of understanding emotionally the fact of the dissolution of the marriage. At the same time the therapist needs to hold out the concept of survival with hope for the future.

The period of the emotional divorce is a chaotic time for the parties as well as a contributing factor to the irrationality exhibited by divorcing people. People still consider themselves as partly married—that is, they still consider themselves in relation to others rather than to "self " (Weiss, 1975, p. 83). They still view their value, worth, or success in terms of their relationship with another person, usually of the opposite sex, rather than being able to view themselves entirely free of the relationship need and as self-worthwhile, alive, and successful in and of themselves, undefined by another person or by their relationship with that person. As the party begins to accept the idea of being single and alone during the transition period, the next period, redirection, begins.

Redirection

The period is marked by different choices being made independently. New values are adopted and made comfortable on the basis of a single life. Life begins new directions. There is a period of overlap between transition and redirection. Few people understand the process of change at the time. However, as in the deliberation period, they are able retroactively to identify the points of change. As this awareness develops, the chances for further meaningful growth become increasingly obvious. How can the mediator determine where a client is along this path? Here is a checklist, based on Federico's work, which indicates stages of growth.

1. People begin by gaining mastery over things they historically disliked doing and always left to the marriage partner. It might be balancing the checkbook or driving on the expressway. This is often the first step. It does not mean that they have outgrown their dislike for doing these things but merely that they have taken a step toward control over their new lives by mastering the skills necessary to do the tasks. The anxiety that earlier worried the clients about whether or not such things could be done are placed behind them. They have "passed the test of self-sufficiency" (Kessler, 1975, p. 43).

2. The client no longer fantasizes about sex with the ex-partner on a regular basis.

3. The client can accept the former partner's remarriage with a workable sense of being able to live with it. Obviously, this is a difficult thing for anyone to deal with at any stage of adjustment. However, being able to accept it and live with it is a major milestone.

4. The client can define her/himself as not only financially okay but also financially secure. This might mean no more than one week's pay in the savings account or it might mean larger sums in more varied ways.

However, the client is going to redefine financial security as s/he moves along the emotional divorce line, and in redefining it reaches another milestone when s/he is able to identify a feeling of self-defined financial security.

5. The client is no longer bitter toward all of the opposite sex. When s/he can begin to distinguish between the marriage partner and all members of the same gender and cease to feel bitter toward all of them, another milestone has been passed.

6. The client reestablishes a normal sexual pattern. The normality is, of course, defined by the client. This can range from the male ceasing to need to attempt to sleep with every woman he comes in contact with (particularly younger women) to overcoming a reluctance to engage in any sex and being able to establish sexual relationships on a comfortable basis.

7. The client no longer overreacts to "trigger" items of the immediate post-divorce period that remind her/him of the marriage. This points up an interesting aspect of the divorce settlement. Many of the items accumulated by a couple over the years of marriage have a special significance. It might be a rocking chair, purchased at a country auction. Every time the person passes that chair, there is a twinge inside, a reminder of the happier days of the marriage. The parties may each want to have that chair and other similar items. Yet having that chair might just serve as a constant chafing to keep the wounds of the dissolution open. The mediator might want to explore with the parties some of the implications of the symbolic meanings of material objects. If they can afford to, the couple may be better off emotionally to discard those particularly significant items of the house rather than to fight over them to see who should get the constant reminder.

The therapist's function

The function of the therapist changes as the clients move through the process. During the deliberation, litigation, and transition periods the clients need a great deal of hand-holding and panic abatement. To this the mediator must add assistance in problem solving. Since there is a great deal of flux between therapy and mediation, the professional will frequently find that s/he can assist in problem solving and goal setting only while engaging in panic abatement and hand-holding.

Thus the four stages of development and the roles of the professional helper can be seen as follows:

	Primary Function of	
Period	*Therapist*	*Mediator*
Deliberation		
	Panic abatement	
Litigation		Problem solving
	Hand-holding	
Transition		
Redirection	Exploring alternative courses of action	Empowerment or developing self-sufficiency skills
	Increasing self-reliance	

If the mediator is successful in her/his role of assisting the clients to problem-solve, set realistic goals, and then achieve them, s/he adds the dimension of empowerment to the redirection period, further enhancing the possibilities of personal growth and increased self-reliance.

Understanding feelings

Almost all divorcing people experience a range of twelve universal feelings. These feelings will often influence the way in which divorcing people think about themselves, their partners, and mediation. Their ability to engage in the give and take of negotiations may be affected by any of these feelings or a combination thereof. While most people experience these feelings, they do not maintain them permanently. If the mediator understands that the feelings are transitional, s/he will not deny them but attempt to use them positively to assist in the mediation. They are as follows.

1. *Rejection* is inherent in every divorce and is basic to everything that follows. Most people conceal their flaws from the world by a range of strategies. However, within the marriage these flaws are slowly revealed to the partner. Therefore, rejection by a partner who understands all the flaws of the other is critical, for it is a rejection of the real self and more damaging than any other form of rejection.

2. *Anger* is generally a secondary emotion (Kessler, 1975, p. 54). That is, it is a reaction to more primary feelings of loss, fear, helplessness, or victimization. The therapist can help the client get in touch with the primary feeling, to define what is causing the anger. Thus s/he can help prevent a recurrence of the same pattern in the future. Anger in the

divorcing situation can be dysfunctional when it is the repetition of the bitterness of the marriage. In this case it adds to the poison of the divorce (Kessler, 1975, p. 37). However, anger can also be functional when it is used as a way of protecting the self from the devastation of separation. It fills the emotional vacuum. If the rejected party cannot reestablish love or caring, at least s/he can cause the ex-spouse enough pain not to be totally ignored or forgotten (Kessler, 1975, p. 39).

   3. *Loneliness*. There is a difference between being lonely and being alone. Loneliness is the fear of nothingness, the feeling that nobody out there cares.

   4. *Confusion* is best characterized by, "What did I do wrong?" The client will have many questions without answers.

   5. *Self-doubt*. The client now hesitates to make decisions because s/he considers the self less capable than before. Frequently s/he also questions competency as wife/mother or husband/father. The sense of self-deprecation may have come out of the "put-downs" of the spouse during marriage or the self-condemnation for having failed in the marriage (Weiss, 1975, p. 76).

   6. *Depression* is a healthy and rational response to divorce. Older people will tend to be less optimistic; they will also feel that they have wasted time on a useless marriage.

   The following three feelings are really fears:

   7. *Fear of making mistakes* in choosing future relationships. There is a tendency to accept the Greek tragedy model in feeling that the next relationship is also preordained to fail because the client has accepted the individual defect model of her/himself.

   8. *Fear of proving inadequate* to life's tasks as a good mother/wife or as a father/provider.

   9. *Fear of going over the edge*, phenophobia. The loss of control, discussed earlier, is often misunderstood as a feeling of craziness, which leads to this fear. It can be diminished by recovering control.

   10. *Anxiety* over the unknown. People worry about whether they can manage financially or maintain their sexual attractiveness; how will the family react? Can they handle all of the things that were previously either mutually handled or dealt with by the spouse? (Kessler, 1975, p. 32).

   11. *Self-pity*. Divorce brings out self-pity in people. It is a natural part of the divorce process and should not necessarily be struggled with as most people get bored with themselves eventually and work through the self-pity period on their own.

   12. *Euphoria* is characterized by intermittent fits of joy to be followed by slumps.

Each of these emotional characteristics of divorcing people will have an impact if displayed during the litigation period. The professional will have to understand them and develop techniques for using them positively to assist in a settlement that helps the parties deal with the crises at the moment and build in arrangements that limit the chances of recurring emotional crises in the future.

In large measure people carry within themselves an inner wisdom. Divorce tends to cut them off from that inner wisdom and the function of the therapist is to reconnect them with their own strengths and inner wisdom. As mediator s/he can help in this reconnection by focusing on the material aspects of the dissolution and by drawing on that inner wisdom to deal with the material assets, hoping to open the way for a reconnection of that inner wisdom in dealing with the emotional aspects as well.

Understanding behavior

Most couples entering divorce mediation will be close to actual separation. Some will have recently separated and will be looking for a way to institutionalize the fact. Others will separate during mediation. The point at which they actually separate will depend on whether they are in the latter part of the deliberation or the early part of the transition stage, two points at which those stages overlap the litigation period.

There are distinctive behaviors in reaction to the actual separation that also appear to be universal and unrelated to the relationship that existed while the couple were living together. That is, people seem to go through similar emotional responses to the separation whether they have just walked out of a violent, angry, or oppressive marriage or whether they have quietly parted by sad, mutual consent. This response can be characterized as the Post-Separation Syndrome and appears in the transition stage. Common behavior reactions of the syndrome include the following:

1. There is a common desire to take a trip to place a physical distance between the self and the marriage. This can be either just an overnight stay at someone's house or a trip to Bermuda and will obviously be shaped by the economics and support systems available.

2. There may be a great interest or disinterest in interpersonal relationships. Divorcing people want companionship and warmth; some will want a heavy relationship with every person they become involved with, while others will go to the other extreme and want a very superficial relationship. This will depend on the way in which each person exhibits the emotions discussed earlier.

3. Some may become sexually hyperactive, others hypoactive. Divorce is followed by a fear of being alone and therefore being inadequate, or of being nothing. This is often dealt with by going to bed with everyone and anyone. Hyperactivity is also an antidote to the feelings of rejection by trying to redeem one's self-worth in other eyes. There are elements of a quasi-marriage in this behavior, i.e., having someone there to wake up with in the morning. Hypoactive persons are engaged in self-pity, fearing a replication of former relationships and therefore studiously avoiding people to whom they are attracted.

Another more complicated behavior pattern of grieving crops up in the transition period and may affect the course of mediation. Its distinctive behavioral components in some ways parallel the loss of a spouse through death. However, there is a qualitative difference between the mourning for a marriage and for a dead spouse. Therefore, the death and dying model of mourning should not be applied directly to divorce. In divorce, the spouse is still alive. In death, the bereaved knows that the spouse is gone forever. Kessler points out that no one is ever totally divorced from a person one has loved deeply (1975, p. 44). Society views widows and divorcees differently; there is sympathy for the widow and society is nonjudgmental about her status, while it is clearly judgmental about the status of a divorced woman.

The divorced person is most likely to be angry with the spouse. The widow is more likely to be angry with fate. The divorcee finds no sympathy and no ritual, for society still ascribes a fault to one or both of the partners in divorce. Finally, in death the deceased is frequently glorified; in divorce the departed is vilified, and the person is aware that s/he, too, is being equally vilified by the other party (Bohannan, 1970, p. 42).

However, a grieving process can be drawn from the death model. That is, a divorced person cannot mourn a death but can and does grieve for a loss, for what died in the divorce died within the griever. It was the loss of a dream of a life together, of a plan for a partnership. It was the loss of a style of life and of a commitment to another person. It was the loss of a definition of one's self as a party to a marriage. This is evidenced by divorced persons tending to empathize rather than sympathize with others going through stress or loss, because they have had to confront unwanted realities. It is also evidenced by a feeling of having wasted a portion of life that cannot be recaptured and is not cherished in memory.

There are qualitatively different experiences for men and women in divorce. The different sexes are apt to have acquired different styles of reacting to stress. Men tend more to act on the world and therefore are less likely to seek therapy. Women are more likely to act on the self and seek inner explanations for the failure of the marriage. This means that there are fewer men in therapy and fewer in group therapy. Weiss quotes the findings of Gerald Gurin and his associates "that 22 percent of separated and divorced men and 40 percent of separated and divorced women had sought professional help for personal problems" (Weiss, 1975, p. 251). Therapists and mediators are less familiar with men's stories. We know more about the women's experiences in divorce. The male story is still largely untold.

After the separation each party experiences different problems. These can be generalized as follows:

Man	Woman
Suffers a loss of purpose—there is no longer a family to support and lead.	Suffers a loss of status.
	Too much to do—a general feeling of being overburdened. At the same time there is a feeling that "something is missing."
There is a need for extra money to set up the new household—it costs $2,500–$5,000 to establish a new apartment.	
	A general feeling of being locked into the children's world, where everything revolves around their needs.
Alone in a new residence, he needs to establish new friends quickly. He has too much free time, therefore feels rootless and has to go out and make things happen. A damaged self-image makes this difficult.	Now needs to work or go to school and subsequently to engage in the world of competitive employment. Very difficult to get out and into a new social life because of the constraints of job/school/home and children and damaged self-image.

An "empty-nest woman" shares problems of both men and women in the younger age group. She has the emptiness of the man's life with the struggle of the woman's.

Another feature of the transition stage is attachment–detachment. A bond develops over time in the marriage so that one person becomes natural in the company of the other. Marriage insures the continued access to the attachment figure (Weiss, 1975, p. 42). Separation raises stress because each party loses the attachment figure. Some people do not experience such stress, however, because the attachment figure is themselves. Therefore, when they are alone they do not experience discomfort. These clients will usually articulate that the marriage was a mistake right from the start. Many couples drift into marriage only to realize quickly that they really did not want to be coupled with the chosen spouse. Thus if there was no investment in the marriage right from the start, no attachment to the other could have taken place. The divorce will seem to be merely "rectifying an error" (Weiss, 1975, p. 16). No detachment is required and the unattached partner will continue to live an unattached life, now simply physically separated from the other.

The goal of the therapist regarding detachment is to assist the couple in developing a sense of self-reliance, confidence, and autonomy for an indefinite period of time, thus allowing them to relate to other people on the basis of warmth, not need. Divorce is, in part, the process of detachment. The detachment process can be measured using the following guidelines. According to Federico (1979), detachment is taking place when

1. clients can admit publicly that they are divorced,
2. there is a clear physical separation from the ex-partner,
3. there is absolutely no sex with the ex-partner,
4. the couple can discard joint belongings,
5. the couple can form a new social network,
6. the parties can develop new romantic interests,
7. the couple are changing their roles with the ex-partner,
8. the couple can complete unfinished business of issues in the marriage that angered, hurt, or disappointed them, but which they were never able to express to the other person.

Detachment can be described as the process of emotional uncoupling or disconnecting. It requires a change from the past to a future orientation: an ability of each person to dream of his or her own independent future (Kessler, 1975, p. 27).

In discussing changing roles it should be noted that the process is usually described only in relation to one person, the ex-partner. The focus should be on more than the changing role in relation to the other party, because as the first relationship changes, so will most other relationships. And if the changing role is a positive experience, growth is enhanced in terms of other relationships. The mediator can assist in changing roles by helping people define their own settlements, which, of necessity, force them to change their roles toward one another.

The last phase to be watched for is the account taking. Part of the redirection process is taking an account of the client's version of how the marriage ended up the way it did. It is not important that each party's account be factually accurate. It can be totally unlike the other partner's view. What is important is that it helps settle issues of who was responsible for what; that, as the account provides a sense of order to the events leading to the breakdown of the marriage, it helps allocate blame among the parties and begins to settle the moral issues of the separation (Weiss, 1975, p. 15).

People can begin to see the paradox of divorce: it is painful but it can be creative, it is full of grief while providing a sense of relief, it is a period of vulnerability but also of self-confidence (Kessler, 1975, p. 81).

Conclusion

Divorce mediation takes place within the emotional context I have outlined above. The mediator not only assists the couple in dissolving their marriage but also helps them to move along the Divorce Adjustment Process at a faster rate and with the minimum of turmoil. If the role of the mediator is understood within the context of the entire emotional process, then s/he can work with the couple, mindful that the way in which the negotiations for a separation agreement are conducted will have an impact on the final settlement. S/he will also be empowering the couple as individuals while easing the pain of the transition period and increasing the potential growth of the redirection period. By adding the role of mediator, the helping professional facilitates smooth movement along an inevitable continuum in an attempt to minimize the emotional damage along the way.

Thus far we have examined the emotional impact of divorce on the parents. In the next chapter we shall examine the emotional impact on the children, along with the difficult issues raised by the presence of children in a divorcing family.

chapter 3

The special problems
of children

The mediator will find that of all the issues in divorce, those surrounding the children—custody, support, and access—are the most contentious. Because the children are the major joint product of the dissolving marriage, the way in which the parents relate to them will have a profound effect on all of the participants' long-term adjustment to the divorce.

When a couple divorce the action changes their status, both legally and emotionally, as husband and wife. However, it does not change their status as father and mother. The children continue to relate to each of them as a parent and to need each of them as a parent (Elkin, 1977, p. 57). Thus the goal in mediation is to help the parents separate the ending of their relationship through the divorce from the rearrangement of the family that the divorce will require (Woolley, 1979, p. 149).

Many parents overlook the permanence of their parental roles during the disruption of their spouse roles. Those parents tend to view the children as objects to be owned. The children are often used as pawns in the negotiations. A major role of the mediator is to limit the "use" of the children and to focus both parties on their permanent roles as parents. In doing so, s/he involves the children in the decision-making process in the belief that they also should be empowered to control their own lives.

It is important to establish the children's role in the talks at the very first session. During the intake process I talk about the children and how the three of us —the couple and I will work together to help make the separation as painless as possible for the children. I point out that research has shown that children get most upset when they do not know what is going on; therefore it is important to be sure that they are aware of the impending changes. I then proceed, "Many children feel responsible in some way for the divorce, and I expect that your kids have some of these feelings; it's natural. One of the things we will want to do is to be sure that the children understand that they were not the cause of the divorce and that they cannot do anything to bring you back together again. If we do that, it will relieve them of the burden of responsibility and prevent them from playing with your lives.

"However, to do that we shall need to involve the children in the negotiations. At the point when we have a basic agreement on the custody, visitation, and support issues we will ask the children to join us so that we can explain everything to them and be sure that we have their agreement on the factors affecting their lives. You probably feel a little apprehensive about this; most parents do. But you will find, as the others did, that it is very helpful. Of course, if the children are teenagers, the courts require that they be consulted about any arrangements made for them, and I know you would also want to do that. So at some point I will tell you when to bring the children in." Since using this approach, I have not had any parent refuse to involve the children at the appropriate point.

Studies indicate that there is a relationship between the amount of turbulence during the deliberation, litigation, and transition periods and the subsequent success during redirection of the parents and adjustment of the children (Hetherington, Cox, & Cox, 1976; Rosen, 1977a & b, 1978a; Wallerstein & Kelly, 1977). Among the factors contributing to the positive adjustment of the children to divorce are (1) minimum conflict between the parents and (2) the frequency of the father's contact with his children.

Rosen shows that it is the level of conflict between the parents rather than the divorce per se which leads to a maladjustment in children (1977a). Wallerstein and Kelly's longitudinal study of children of divorcing parents indicates that the young child's adjustment to the divorce is influenced by the relationship between the parents during the entire post-separation period, not just by the conflict preceding the divorce or the divorce itself (1977).

Alternative custody options

Most people come to divorce mediation believing that single-parent custody with tightly regulated visitation rights is the only choice open to them. They are angry with one another, and the formal custody–visitation arrangements provide a structure for dealing with their anger. Hetherington and associates (1976) found that most divorced parents are consumed by the relationship between the ex-spouse and the children. More than that, they found that two-thirds of the exchanges between couples in the immediate post-divorce period involve conflicts (p. 17). However, when the couple were in agreement and supported each other, despite the divorce, the whole family suffered less disruption than in high-conflict situations. This was accompanied by an earlier return to normal family functioning (p. 31).

This relationship between the amount of conflict or turbulence and the adjustment of the children to the divorce suggests that if the mediator can offer the couple a range of options that lead to greater parental cooperation and support, s/he not only helps ease the marriage dissolution but also strengthens the new family arrangements that emerge from the divorce.

I attempt to do this through a set of sample clauses that focus not on custody (which I define as the physical location of the child) but on parental responsibilities. I discuss with both parents the children's need for each of them. I help the parents see that the way in which they will deal with each other in the immediate future in regard to their children will, in large measure, determine how their children will relate to them over an even longer period of time.

There is no single arrangement that fits all families. Custody arrangements will vary from family to family, depending on incomes, life-styles, work, and the nurturing abilities of each parent. Thus the mediator helps the couple choose the arrangement most suitable to their particular set of needs. "Where parents honestly choose the best arrangement, most realistic for them, their children stand the best chance at a healthy adjustment" (Ramos, 1979, p. 63).

Most couples I have seen arrive with a general, predetermined idea of what the arrangements for the children will be. Either the children go with the mother and the issues for negotiation are support and visitation; or the parties have decided to use the children as pawns and the issue is which parent will become the custody parent.

Some parents are too involved in the struggle with the partner to be able to see the children's interests. In this situation the children become pawns in the overall fight. It is important for the mediator to be able to devise strategies to help the parents see when they are using the children.

In the latter instance I begin by exploring what visitation rights each parent is looking for and lay out the content of the key agreement clauses.[1] In the process I explore whether the parents are interested in having visitation rights for themselves or whether they want the children to have access to them as parents. Most parents have not thought about what the children want in terms of access (Metz, 1968, p. 93).

To help them do this, I suggest that the couple think of themselves as co-parents (Bohannan, 1970, p. 52) and keep room(s) open at all times for the use of the children. The noncustody parent will probably not have

---

[1] They relate to custody tempered by the parents' equal rights in bringing up the children; parental cooperation in these matters; agreement to consult on all major decisions affecting the children; keeping living arrangements open in both households for the children; arrangements for vacations; limiting gifts to under $25 in value, unless they are given jointly. The full text of these clauses is included in the sample agreement in Appendix B.

thought of that arrangement, and, if s/he agrees to it, the economic feasibility of such living space will have to be considered as part of the total economic arrangements of the separation. The custody parent will also respond to this clause, because it opens the possibility of the children's making a choice. If the parent's response is hostile, I try to develop an inventory of advantages and disadvantages in such an open arrangement. On the disadvantage side I list the arguments just raised by the party. On the advantage side I discuss the burdens of custody. In addition to being deemed the more nurturing of the pair and therefore possibly the more wanted, the custody parent also gets to stay up nights when the child has flu. The custody parent's life continues to be defined by the needs of the children; an evening out becomes a major event by the time a baby sitter is found and paid for.

Access versus visitation

I point out that some of these burdens can and should be shared by the noncustody spouse. However, such sharing will require an accommodation to the structured custody–visitation pattern. Raising these alternatives helps to get the person thinking more about the future without the spouse and how s/he will handle this single-parent role.

On the other side, the noncustody parent may at first not want to provide more than visitation rights for her/himself. In this case I point out (usually to him) that his best interests are served if his wife is able to develop a new life independent of him. Her independence, through employment or remarriage, may reduce his alimony obligation and, there-fore, he should assist in his wife's development. This requires that she be free from the children for full weekends and have some evenings out. The only way she can do this is if he has the children. Thus giving the children greater access to the noncustody father is in the father's long-term interest as an ex-husband. The Milton and Jane case in which Milton finally agreed to take the boys for a few weekends a year is an example of this type of intervention (Chapter 6).

In the process of these discussions I turn the focus from custody and visitation to access and joint responsibility, from the present litigation-transition period to the future redirection. I use the following three access definitions developed by Rosen in her work with children of divorce (Rosen, 1977a):

Free access means unrestricted contact between child and the non-custodial parent. As long as the children are preteenagers, both parents must live within reasonable distance of each other. Reasonable, in this context, is defined by the children's needs. It also requires that the custody parent encourage and support the children's continued close involvement with the noncustody parent. This raises another issue, namely, to what extent does the freedom of access of the noncustody parent to the children in the home of the custody parent limit the freedom of the custody parent? Many women who have custody are unwilling to permit the father to drop in whenever he pleases, for this means that she must regulate her life to the possibility of his presence.

Regulated access spells out the time duration and place of contact with the noncustody parent. In most cases the noncustody parent picks up the children and takes them out. Occasionally, the custody parent leaves home while the noncustody parent visits.

Occasional access has no set pattern. The noncustody parent sees the children sporadically. When this occurs because the noncustody parent is reluctant to have closer or more frequent contact, the task of the mediator is to try to build in more frequent contact as the basis of relief for the custody parent.

Most children experience suffering and intense longing for the absent parent, which is eased by increased access to that parent (Wallerstein & Kelly, 1977, p. 13). The children's response to this pain is fairly predictable according to age and the extent to which they are aware of the reasons for the divorce. (This point repeats itself in each of the reports published by Wallerstein and Kelly.) Therefore the mediator tries to share this observation with the parents in a way that facilitates their understanding of the need to arrive at a reasonable arrangement concerning the children. The couple need to acknowledge that the children have a right to a relationship with both parents (Suarez, Weston, & Hartstein, 1978, p. 277).

When arrangements are thought of in terms of access, the decisions around joint custody can be more clearly understood. Joint legal custody should be distinguished from joint physical custody (Wheeler, 1980, p. 61). The former does not require that both parents live close to one another or that they have relatively equal incomes. It merely requires that they share with the other the decision-making responsibilities around their children's futures and growth. Joint legal custody is my goal in suggesting the series of clauses that enable the spouses to share in the parenting and upbringing.

On the other hand, joint physical custody requires that the parents continue to live in close proximity to each other so that the children spend part of the week with one parent and part with the other. A variation of this is an arrangement where the children spend weekdays with one parent and weekends with the other. Yet another way is for the children to stay in the original house and for each of the parents to move in and out in turn. Successful joint physical custody requires that the parents live in the same neighborhood so that the children can continue to attend the same school, develop and maintain relationships with one set of peers, and maintain a stable life-style. This in turn requires that both parents enjoy a relatively equal income. Residential areas are usually economically homogeneous, and if both parents are to have apartments in the same part of town, they will pay approximately the same rent. If they choose to live in a suburban area, they will require similar houses. Since equal incomes are rare, I do not believe that joint physical custody is broadly applicable from the economic perspective. There is, however, another problem that needs understanding. When spouses divorce they are beginning to develop independent lives as separate people. A mediator who helps a couple achieve an agreement for joint physical custody should explore, first, whether the couple really want to develop independent, separate lives and, second, whether their desire for joint physical custody and the limitation it places on them by forcing them to live in the same neighborhood, shop at the same stores, and function within the same general social setting, may not be a statement about their unreadiness to divorce.

It is my general viewpoint that parents should be encouraged to share in joint legal custody, which protects the parenting rights of both. At the same time access to the children should be as flexible as possible so as to help maintain the parent–child ties.

If this is done successfully, the need for joint physical custody is minimized and placed in an appropriate context. Both parents can think about living in situations that promote their independent development, because their roles and rights as parents are protected.

Involving the children

In addition to the reasons stated earlier for involving the children, they are less likely to feel a need to have to choose between the parents, when they see their parents talking to each other openly about them. They are then free to have a relationship with both of them (Suarez, Weston, & Hartstein, 1978, p. 280).

Parents are universally reluctant to explain the reasons for the divorce to their children (Bohannan, 1970, p. 56). The younger the children, the less likelihood of the parents' sharing information with them; 80 percent of the parents of preschool children found the "task too difficult" (Wallerstein & Kelly, 1977, p. 13). Although the percentage of children who share in some understanding of the divorce increases with their age, there is still a large gap between parent and child perceptions. "Only 45% of the children considered that their parents had given them a satisfactory explanation of the divorce" (Rosen, 1978a, p. 2).

Since we know that understanding the divorce will ease the problems for the children, and adequate access diminishes the distress of separation, it is important to engage the children in the divorce mediation process.

Measuring parental commitment

When the issue of custody presents itself as a tough, highly disputable block, I ask each of the parents to complete three tasks:

1. to make an inventory of the reasons the children should be with them,
2. to list what accommodations they are willing to make about the way they handle the children to make it possible for the other party to agree to her/his having custody,
3. to list what accommodations the other party would have to make about the way s/he handles the children to make it possible for the responder to agree to the other spouse's having custody.

When the couple return with the lists, a review of the statements gives me some insight as to which parent really wants custody. Usually one list contains more nurturing items and the corresponding accommodations sought from the partner are few and contrived. The parent who is using custody as a negotiating tool provides a list that emphasizes non-nurturing reasons for having the children. But corresponding accommodations will include real items of change s/he wants in the partner's handling of the children.

Children, by and large, tend to be the victims of the circumstances surrounding the divorce. The extent to which the mediator can remove some of the exacerbating circumstances—poor communications, high parental turbulence, rejection, or use of the children as pawns—will determine the future adjustment of the children and the speed and effectiveness with which the parents move from the transition to the redirection period.

Goals for the mediator

When working with families the mediator has a set of goals that help to frame his/her values. Among those goals are an uncoupling of the spouses in a way that leaves no victims, allows the couple open lines of communication between themselves, and provides each child with a direct and open line of communication to each parent. Thus any arrangement that would victimize a person in that family would be unacceptable to the mediator. The solutions the mediator works for are family solutions.

The goal of leaving the family with clear and open lines of communication in which to develop their new family constellations can be implemented during the times that the children are involved in the negotiations. In the following case I helped the family develop new ways of communicating with each other, which, in turn, developed new structures for that family system, even as it divided. I did that by involving both partners in both the overt and covert intentions of the strategies. The outcome was a new way for the children to relate to each of the parents, which left them with direct lines of communication; it also demonstrates the care the mediator must take to assure that all negotiations take place in a win–win context. That is, each party must have a win in each compromise so that in letting go, the compromise is not seen as a loss. Finally, the result demonstrates a way to engage the children in the negotiations and to link their emotional needs with their financial futures.

The case of Gary and Ruby

Gary and Ruby's marriage had been stormy. Ruby, a devout evangelical Catholic, could not tolerate Gary's gambling and drinking. The more Gary went off with the boys, the deeper Ruby became involved in her religion, taking the two teenage daughters with her. Gary, who was resigned to the divorce, had only one regret: he did not have the relationship with Julia and June that he secretly wanted. As they became more evangelical, along with their mother, his opportunity to get closer to them diminished.

In the economic negotiations the couple were able to work out most of the issues. However, they were apart on the amount and duration of support. Despite protracted negotiations and many attempts on my part, they were still $125 a month apart. At this point I decided to link the parent–child relationship with the economic support issue. I suggested that it was time to bring the children into the negotiations, and that we first talk about access and visitation. It seemed to me that the girls ought to be able to work those issues out in direct negotiations with the father. I discussed the various options with both parents.

In addition, I discussed with each parent separately the idea that if the children were to develop a better relationship with both parents, we ought to try to build into the agreement systematic arrangements that provide a vehicle for better father–daughter relationships. I suggested that if we could work out the access–visitation issue, perhaps we should then add another item for a daughter–father discussion: i.e., money. Both daughters needed money for clothes and their social lives. If this money was to come out of the support figures the parents were talking about, there would be very little available. Thus, if the children could work out a direct relationship with the father for a personal and clothing allowance, this would help achieve two goals. It could be the way of closing the gap between the spouses regarding the amount of money support, and it would also establish a continuing functional link between the father and daughters that could be built upon as the basis for a permanent relationship independent of the mother. I planned to try to develop the idea that the father would give the daughters clothing money in addition to the amount he was already willing to give to the wife for their support.

This was not an easy task, since it meant engaging the mother in this strategy so that she did not see these direct father–child talks as circumventing her, or undermining the special alliance she had developed with the younger daughter. I laid out the goals to Ruby, explaining the pros and cons. I first sought her feelings about the father's relationship with the children. Ruby agreed it was not good and she expressed the wish that it could be improved. I developed some ideas on the consequences of this new relationship. I pointed out that it could mean that they would grow closer to him, but that this would not necessarily mean they would drift away from her. I indicated, however, that the alliance with her younger daughter might change if the daughter had an independent relationship with the father. While doing this I raised the possibility of direct support payments to the children as a way of increasing the total amount of money she would receive.

Ruby thought it over. She was unable to agree at that session. She needed time to think about it. At the beginning of the following session I again spent some time with her alone. She had some questions about the money aspects. We clarified the issue so that if Gary paid the girls a clothing allowance, it would have to be sufficient to cover all of their clothing needs. We explored the benefits to be gained by Ruby from the children's better relationship with their father. We explored further how Ruby could give up some of the less welcome discipline issues and how it was her right to have some weekends free while the children were with Gary. As she worked through these questions she became more receptive to the idea, finally giving me the OK to proceed with this plan of action.

I then met with Gary and explored his feelings about the barrier that existed between him and the girls. He resented having to go through the mother for any contact with his daughters, but he was not sure how he could break through what he saw as a solid wall of opposition. I raised the possibility of his developing a direct relationship through negotiating with the girls about when and how they would visit together. He doubted that

Ruby would allow that. I suggested that we give it a try. He liked the idea of the direct talks. We then turned to the support issue. I began by asking him how the girls got their clothes. He said that Ruby made some and that she took the girls shopping for other things. He said that on odd occasions the girls had asked him for money for a pair of shoes. I asked him how he had felt when they did that. He said that it had pleased him, and that if he had the money, he would try to take them shopping. Obviously, he enjoyed that contact.

I then raised the possibility that he might also like to negotiate directly with the girls over a clothing allowance. He could figure out with them how much they would need over a year and could agree to give them that allowance, either directly in cash or by taking them shopping and paying the bill up to an agreed-upon amount. Again, he doubted that Ruby would allow it. I asked him if he would like to give it a try. He said he would. I raised the possibility with him that Ruby might try to sabotage those talks unless she also had a stake in the positive outcome. I reminded him of the win–win strategies we had talked about earlier and said that if the clothing allowance was not deducted from the amount he was already offering to Ruby for support, she would have a strong incentive to help achieve a positive outcome. He mulled this over and finally agreed it was worth a try, and we asked Ruby to join us. The three of us then set a date for the children to come in and laid out the ground rules for these talks.

I said that I would direct the conversation and that I would try to establish a direct channel of communication between the father and the daughters. I indicated that this would not be easy and said that if I found that either Gary or Ruby were falling back into their old ways regarding the girls, I would intervene and get the talks back on track. I explained that I would probably be much more actively directive in the session with the children than usual. The parents accepted this and left, prepared for the next session.

The following week Gary and Ruby arrived together with Julia and June. As I ushered them into the room I arranged the seating so that the two girls faced their father. I wanted them to be able to talk directly to him. I opened by thanking the girls for coming and by recognizing their apprehension about what might happen. I then launched immediately into a discussion about their parents' decision to separate, pointing out that this meant that they were divorcing as husband and wife but would always remain father and mother to them. I told the girls how much both parents loved them and I shared with them some of the feelings each parent had expressed about them to me. As I did this, the girls threw careful glances to the mother to see what her reaction would be. She nodded assent during most of my talk.

I then pointed out to them that while this situation must be very difficult for them as young women, it also presented them with an opportunity to change their relationship with their father. I asked them what they wanted from their father: when did they want him to visit them, when did they want to visit him, what kind of things did they want? Again, they both looked to the mother for clearance. I told them that Ruby and I had discussed this and that she too wanted them to have a better relationship with their father, and one of her ways of showing her love for them was not to deprive them of a father. The eldest began, "Well, I wish he would come when he says he's coming." She dropped her gaze to the carpet.

"I see; sometimes Dad promises to come and then doesn't show?"

"Yes."

"Now, have you ever told him that directly?"

"No."

"Do you think you could?"

"Yes."

"Good. Now, swing your chair around just a little and face your father directly. Tell him, while looking at him, what you feel about those plans. Gary, while Julia is talking, swing your chair around slightly and look directly at Julia . . . that's right. OK, Julia, tell him."

"Last week you said you were coming over Sunday afternoon to go skating and then we were going out for supper and you didn't come. You just left a message with Mom to say you wouldn't make it. And that hurt."

"Which part hurt the most, Julia, the fact that Dad didn't come or the fact that he didn't tell you directly?"

"Both, but mostly the fact that he didn't even call us, he just left a message with Mom."

"Gary, how does that feel? Don't tell me. Talk directly to Julia."

"Well, the reason I couldn't come was that my car broke down. But I didn't realize that you would be upset about my not talking to you directly. Anyway, I didn't get a chance to talk to you. Mom answered the phone and I began to tell her my problem with the car, when she said she'd heard that story before and hung up."

"You didn't call back and ask to speak to Julia or June directly?"

"No, I didn't think of it."

Ruby interjected that she then had had to deal with the girls who, as a result, were difficult to live with that afternoon. I asked Ruby to hold onto that point and turned again to Julia.

"Julia, what would you like to have happen if a similar problem crops up in the future? Don't tell me. Tell your Dad."

"Well, I'd like him to tell me himself. Because perhaps we could've figured out a way of meeting somewhere in the middle by bus."

"OK, speak directly to Dad; what would you like to happen?"

"Dad, I wish you would talk to me directly instead of always leaving messages with Mom."

Gary began to realize that he could talk to the girls directly and that it might be better for him if he did. I turned to Ruby, anxious to pick up on her earlier comment and help her understand the double cost of Gary's dealing with the girls through her. It reduced her to a messenger who only carried the bad news. I then focused on the girls reactions and the fact that when this happened, they took it out on Ruby for the rest of the day. I wanted to try to reinforce this new way of family interaction by focusing on the individual benefits to be gained from such a change. At this point I asked June what she thought. "Do you agree with your sister?"

"Up to a point. I don't care if he leaves messages with Mom, I trust her to give them to us, but I do object to giving up an afternoon with my friends to be with my father who then cancels out on me."

"That's a fair point. Why don't you tell Dad directly."

We again moved the chairs to the best opposite locations, persuaded Gary and June to look directly at one another and June repeated her point. Gary shifted uncomfortably on the chair. He was less able to take this criticism from the younger daughter but, following as it did the script of the elder, he had to deal with it in the same way.

Ruby was obviously nervous about the outcome of these talks. She was concerned that her special relationship with the girls would be undermined as their new relationship with the father developed. I was worried that she would find a way of sabotaging the finalization of these talks. I suggested that we have a short separate session where I could explore some of these issues with her. The other three waited outside. I alerted Ruby to the fact that she would probably find some way during the week to prevent any further discussions from taking place. It seemed that she would need a clear focus if she was to be able to permit her daughters to deal directly with the husband. I explored her fears. She was, of course, still angry with Gary and annoyed at the thought that he might be rewarded for the divorce by developing a better relationship with the girls. On the other hand, a deeper fear emerged. What would happen if the girls developed a better relationship with him than they had with her? Might they choose to go with him in a year or so? If that happened, what would it mean for her in terms of support? Gary's support offer to her was predicated on child support, not alimony. If the girls left before she was on her feet, would she be left without the girls and without any financial support? We explored these issues and tried to place them in the context of her growth and the freedom that would come to her if the girls were less dependent on her.

During the week I received a phone call from the husband, saying that he had not been to visit his daughters because when he called to say he was coming, he found that the wife's sister was there. They had all told me about the animosity between Ruby's sister and Gary. I asked Gary if he had talked to the girls. He said he had and had left the next visit open. I then suggested that he call the girls again and go to the house, or arrange to take them out to dinner so that they could talk. He agreed to give it another try. They did indeed meet and work out a schedule of visits, an arrangement of each notifying the other if something came up that would prevent the visit, and a general agreement on the kind of things that they might do. They worked out a joint visit twice a month and the other two weeks he would go out with each daughter separately. That way each would get some undivided "daddy" time.

At the next session with the family Gary was glowing. Ruby was unsettled and I thought it might be useful to try to produce a win for her before moving on to the next part of the negotiations between the father and daughters. I asked Gary whether he had talked to the girls about what they needed in the way of an allowance for clothes. He said they had not really talked about it, but that he would like to. At this point I suggested that if he would like to talk about it, we should do so today. However, we should first get an agreement between the spouses on one important aspect: that if Gary indeed did come to a separate arrangement with the girls over money, it would not affect their current positions regarding support. Gary asked for clarification. I explained that they each had a figure on the table.

"You are currently talking about giving Ruby $450 a month, right?"
"Yes."
"And Ruby says it costs her at least $600 a month, right?"
"Yes."
"Now, if you talk to the girls about money and come to an agreement with them about their clothing needs, you cannot come back and drop your $450 figure; agreed?" Gary thought about it for a moment and agreed. I then turned to the girls and said, "OK, it's now time to talk about money with your father, but you must understand that as you do this you are not taking any money away from your mother for the basic cost of living at home. And, Ruby, you are clear, I hope, that these talks between Gary and the girls do not affect your negotiations with Gary over support."

"Right," she replied.

"OK, let's use the same rules that we had last week. You two talk directly to Dad about what you need in clothing and regular allowance. If you need help from Mom to remember how much you spent last year on clothes, that's OK. You can ask her. But you must speak directly to Dad on the actual issue. Who wants to begin?" They looked at each other and then to the mother and then back to each other. "How about looking at your Dad," I suggested. "Do you have trouble remembering how much you might need?" They both nodded in assent. "Then try to approach it from another angle. You are both teenagers and probably each can make a little extra money from babysitting. What things do you think you ought to buy out of your own pocket money and what sort of things do you think your father should buy?"

This focused on a definition rather than a negotiation, and each daughter could begin to work on that. They discussed this primarily between themselves, at first self-conscious of the fact that they were doing all of this in front of both parents. However, they slowly reached an agreement on the kinds of things they should pay for—basically the nonessentials. In this they sought and received help from Ruby as to what fell in what category. Finally they were ready to deal directly with their father. They presented a principle that he should buy the things on list A—necessities—and they should pay for any items on list B—the non-necessities. I then suggested that they talk about the two lists in general terms. They quickly reached an agreement that Gary would finance their basic clothes purchases. Gary then asked, "But how much will this cost me?" I said it would cost him whatever he finally agreed to pay, and that one way of controlling the costs was to set an upper limit. They haggled for a while on how much this should be. The kids tried to push their father's figure up, and he had trouble deciding what was appropriate. At one point I suggested the girls check with their mother as to what was a reasonable figure, and Ruby came in on Gary's side and a monthly figure was agreed upon. They agreed to keep a running account, so that over the course of the year they would not expect Gary to spend more than twelve times the monthly rate.

At the end of these talks I asked the girls to step outside to the waiting room, because I wanted to build on the brief cooperation between Gary and Ruby. As soon as the kids left the room, I turned to Ruby and said, "That was very helpful of you to support Gary on the figure the kids really needed. I suspect that if you had not been there to help, he may have been hit with a much higher bill." She smiled and Gary turned to her and said "Yeah, thanks." I built on the previous cooperation by refocusing the couple on the one outstanding issue—the difference between the two support figures. Ruby was now ready to move off the $600 figure, and she indicated that she would modify her demand in response to what Gary had done. Gary, who still felt good about the talks with the girls, agreed that he could go higher on his figure and they quickly reached an agreement.

I asked the girls to rejoin us and while all four were together, reviewed the overall terms of the agreement. That way everyone knew what was in the final package, and the girls knew exactly where they would stand in the future. The consequence of not involving the children in the negotiations can be broken agreements or further negotiations *with* the children. The Bea and Ben case (see Chapter 6 p. 100) demonstrates this problem.

part II

The mediation process

chapter 4

Factors affecting
the process

An effective divorce mediator spends considerable time preparing for the
negotiations. Indeed, the actual face-to-face bargaining is the final, and
often shortest, part of the process. However, s/he must be aware of a
number of factors that will affect the outcome of mediation.

These factors are (1) the source of referral, which often determines
the client's position on the Divorce Adjustment Process scale; (2) the
blockages that develop in the negotiations and that can be signals to the
mediator to refer the client back to the referring therapist and/or to go back
to therapy; and (3) the power relationships in the marriage that will impact
the ability of the couple to negotiate. These factors need to be considered
before discussing the implementation of the model.

Referral

Couples come to the mediator in one of three ways. One or both have been
in therapy with the mediator or another therapist, they have been referred
by an external source, or they are self-referred specifically for mediation.

The original therapist should be able to locate the couple's position
on the Divorce Adjustment Process scale. When the therapist and
mediator are co-workers, this is easily accomplished by a conference at the
time of referral. The referral from an external source usually places the full
responsibility for locating the couple's Divorce Adjustment Process position on the mediator.

When the clients are already in therapy with a co-worker, the best
way for the mediator to start is to join the couple and the therapist, to be
introduced by the therapist, and to do part of the intake process with the
therapist present. As a relationship between the couple and the mediator
begins to be established, the therapist leaves, and the mediation process
begins. This appears to work best by having the therapist schedule the
couple for a double session and having the mediator join the therapy

session at the thirty-minute mark. When this formal transition process is not available, the mediator must establish the relationship unaided.

When the clients are transferred to the mediator from a co-therapist, they should be screened carefully to ensure that the transfer is taking place because they want a divorce, not because the therapist has reached a block in her/his relationship. (The Sheila and Marvin and Ira and Bev cases in Chapter 6 are examples of premature referral.)

It appears that an external referral, which requires independent initiative on the part of the couple to seek out the mediator, is a good readiness indicator. Couples who seek out mediation are more apt to be ready for it and to have worked out the major emotional blocks. (The Jack and Jean case in Chapter 6 is an example of self-referral.)

Blockages

Regardless of the source of the referral, the mediator will encounter clients who are not ready for divorce and who should not be in mediation. Such clients will probably send out signals that should be picked up by the mediator.

One of the signals for which the mediator should watch is the man (usually) who balks at the fee. Since the cost of mediation is significantly lower than an attorney's fee, and most clients know this, there is a good chance that a husband who protests the fee and wants it substantially reduced, or even eliminated, does not want to go through with the divorce.

Another signal might involve the denial by either party that they are here for divorce. This could be expressed by such a statement as, "I thought we were just going to separate for a trial," or, "I'm not interested in a divorce." Even though one party is clear about wanting a divorce, this reluctance by the other party must be identified by the mediator as either an unreadiness to enter divorce mediation or as a negotiating tactic. If it is the latter, the mediator deals with it later in the process.

One form of resistance that emerges early in the process is a refusal to accomplish an assigned task, such as budgeting for separate households. The mediator must confront the reluctant party about any of these signals and be prepared to suggest to the clients that they return to therapy or marriage counseling, unless the mediator is clear that divorce is certain and both parties are ready for it. When the mediator determines that the couple are not ready for mediation, s/he should refer them back to the therapist for further counseling.

If the mediator does not make this referral to the therapist, s/he will become an additional therapist to the couple. In the Bev and Ira case, I felt that I became the third therapist. Bev was seeing her therapist once a week, Ira was seeing a different counselor, and they both came to me for a weekly joint session of therapy.

Power relationships

I have observed that one of the two divorcing people usually exercises more power than the other. I believe that there are three primary power positions that affect the mediation process. They are (1) the power to control the income; (2) the power to reject the other partner; and (3) the power to resist a settlement.

Power to control the income

Income control is probably the most complex of the power relationships. Obviously the income producer will have considerable power in any relationship. Thus, if the husband is the sole income producer, he will exercise power over the wife, who will enter the negotiations with the fear of losing this income source. This fear is mitigated as the husband's and wife's incomes equalize.

This power relationship is further complicated when either party is unaware of the exact income. It is surprising how many women do not know the exact amount of their husband's pay check. On the other hand, I have also seen a number of cases where the family earned income "off the books." Either the husband earned commissions that were paid in a separate check, or the wife had a small business and did not maintain precise accounts. When this situation arises, the mediator's task is made more difficult because the problem of power relationships around money is clouded by the existence of income, which, at least in the early stages, neither party is willing to identify clearly.

No matter what the size of the income, the threat of taking it away will generate considerable fear in either party. The husband and wife will also experience fear about changes in income management that will result from the separation, because once the income has been produced, another set of power relationships will emerge over how the money is going to be handled. There are four ways in which money is managed in most households:

1. The husband handles all financial transactions.
2. The wife handles all financial transactions.

3. The wife handles the weekly transactions, food shopping, cleaners, clothing, etc., while the husband manages the monthly or quarterly transactions, mortgage payments, auto and life insurance, investments, etc.
4. Both partners share in handling all financial matters.

In those family situations where one spouse handles all financial transactions, the other will feel considerable anxiety about his/her ability to take over this chore. In situations where the money has been handled on a split basis (No. 3), both partners will experience anxiety about their ability to manage the other's part. The husband, even though he is the income producer, will be afraid of having to handle the weekly chores of shopping and managing the house. Since he has no idea how to do it, the prospect of setting up a separate household will not be welcome, and he will probably compensate for his uncertainty by wanting to keep a larger share of the income.

The wife may know how to handle the weekly household management but will experience anxiety about handling the insurance agents and the bank on a quarterly basis. Only those couples who have shared financial responsibilities in the past will be able to deal with the new arrangements without undue anxiety over the unknown.

The mediator's role in this situation is to help the parties break the broad economic problems into manageable components, so that each may share with the other the power they derive from the control of that knowledge. Usually this will mean helping the husband share the basic income data with the wife, which enables the mediator to explore with her the available options that flow from this understanding.

At the same time the mediator, through the use of the budget materials, helps the husband understand the ramifications of daily household management, hopefully in a way that demystifies it. In facilitating a sharing of knowledge between the husband and wife, the mediator helps to equalize the power relationships in the negotiations.

Power of rejection

The second part of power relates to which of the two parties wants the divorce. The party who wants out of the marriage has the power of rejection. Even in cases in which, at the time of intake, the decision to divorce appears mutual, it would be safe to assume that one party initiated that decision and therefore still has that power advantage over the other. The rejected party will normally hold on to the departing spouse in an attempt to stop the rejection.

The mediator can help the reluctant party to understand the reality of the divorce and the effect of her/his behavior on the spouse, and share the knowledge that pleading to hang on to a marriage the other partner does not want gives the rejecting partner considerable power in the negotiations. The mediator does this during the early sessions devoted to defining short- and long-term goals.

The Jane and Milt case is a good example of this. Milt was overly concerned about maintaining his youth. The breakdown of the marriage began after the birth of the second child, when Milt found a younger woman. For six months he refused to have sexual relations with his wife, because he had this other woman. However, his sense of values also prevented him from telling his wife why he refused to sleep with her.

Thus Jane was doubly rejected. First, she was rejected in the marriage by the husband, wondering what she had done to cause this break in conjugal relations. Second, she was rejected when she learned that the reason for the break was that Milt had found another woman. Short of finding some magical youth potion, there was little Jane could do to avoid this crisis. Milt, because of his own unmet needs, reached out for his passing youth through a much younger woman. Jane could only watch.

In the negotiations Jane was always afraid of making demands. Milt was offering generous settlement terms. However, she was plagued by the idea that he could reject her—and the children—again by cutting off the money supply. She was able to frame her demands and articulate them directly to Milt only after she understood that she did indeed have power: the power to resist a settlement and the divorce that Milt wanted.

Jane and Milt came to mediation from family therapy. While all of the problems of the relationship and the divorce had not been worked out, Jane had sufficient insights before entering mediation for me to give her an understanding of her power to equalize the relationship.

Looking at this case—a relatively young couple with two small children and considerable affection by the wife toward the husband—it would be natural to question whether they were indeed ready for divorce. If they had not been referred by a therapist who already had worked through a number of issues with them, I would have turned them back to the family therapist to determine their readiness.

Because of the source of the referral, however, I was able to avoid trying to patch up this marriage, which would have been a destructive move on my part. I was able to concentrate on the role of the mediator as an assistant in dissolving the marriage, not putting it back together again.

To be sure that the couple have indeed passed the point of no return in their marriage places a great onus on the mediator. The answer can often be found in a discussion with the referring therapist. If the referral is not totally clear, or if the couple arrive without a referral, it is incumbent on the mediator to examine the readiness issue with the couple in the first few sessions.

Once this issue is clear, the mediator can look at ways to help make the decision to divorce mutual. The rejected party must first deal with the issue of rejection and then begin to identify the strengths and talents that have often been submerged by or during the marriage. If the future is being considered only in terms of how difficult it will be to make ends meet, the insecurity of the rejected party will be heightened.

However, if the focus is on the new person who can grow and develop out of the dissolution, the possibility of reaching an agreement is enhanced. That is why I believe it is important to place a heavy emphasis on the spouse's independence. For the wife this often means focusing on further education or training, or on child-care arrangements that will enable her to return to work. The mediator opens new options for the wife (assuming she is the rejected party) that can help her focus on the future with new possibilities rather than new insecurities.

When the husband is the rejected party, similar efforts need to be made to focus on a future independent from the wife. At the same time the mediator would emphasize the father's access to the children as a way of limiting the rejection to that of the wife and not also of the children.

Power of resistance

Finally, there is the power of resistance. This power is unique to mediated divorces. When the couple chooses to litigate their divorce, the attorneys usually attempt to negotiate a settlement. Any unresolved issues will be brought to court, where the judge will probably hear some of the arguments and then send the parties out to try again to reach a negotiated settlement. If one party still resists reaching an agreement, they all will have to come back into the court where the judge—acting as arbitrator—imposes a decision on the couple. At that point the power to resist is removed.

In mediation a party may resist reaching an agreement if, contrary to the referral, s/he is not really ready to divorce. The resistance is expressed as a refusal to come to a final agreement on *any* of the issues. The cases of Marvin and Sheila and Bev and Ira are examples of a resistant spouse preventing an agreement and therefore the divorce.

In the cases I have dealt with, the resistant party has usually been the rejected one, and it may well be that an inability to deal with that rejection leads to the resistance that blocks a divorce. When the resistance is high, it is often useful for the mediator to share her/his observations with the couple. I identify to the couple ways in which the resistance is preventing a settlement and then go on to suggest that neither partner has completely examined the reasons for the divorce. I suggest that we might take "time out" from the mediation to look at what each party did not get out of the marriage that s/he wanted as a way of looking at what each now wants to get out of the future. If each party knows what s/he did not get out of the marriage, it is easier to let go of the relationship. If the resistant party senses that the time-out is to be marriage counseling, s/he will quickly reject the offer. However, if both spouses recognize that the time-out of mediation will help them arrive at a separation agreement more easily, they are likely to accept it.

Once the couple agree to spend time looking at the reasons for the breakup, I contract for a specific number of sessions, usually one session to focus on the husband, another to focus on the wife, and possibly a third to try to draw some implications from these two sessions. I usually begin with the rejected partner. Assuming it is the husband, I begin with the question, "What is it that, as a man, you did not get from your relationship with (the spouse)?" I reframe this question in a number of ways, encouraging the resistant partner to articulate her/his complaints about the other. I try to keep the spouse out of this exploration, focusing on one partner. Occasionally I will turn to the other, indicate I know it is tough to keep quiet for this long and thank him/her for cooperating. As the reluctant partner begins to identify and articulate to the mediator those things about the spouse that s/he disliked, s/he begins to develop the strength to reject the spouse. In the process, the rejection becomes mutual and, by making it mutual, the power relationship is equalized.

It is possible that, as each partner identifies the problems s/he has with the other, one or both indicate that they would like to explore these *they* issues further. This should be encouraged and the couple should be referred back to the original therapist or to another family therapist to work on those issues. If they work them out successfully, they will restore the balance to the marriage and begin to develop a new relationship while remaining married. If they do not resolve their differences, they will at least return to mediation more ready to negotiate the real issues. I believe that it is inappropriate for the mediator to work with the couple as a therapist for more than a couple of time-out sessions. Couples requiring more intensive therapy should be referred back to the referring therapist.

Comparison with labor mediation

There are many factors that differentiate divorce mediation from labor mediation. While there is often real anger felt by one or both parties in labor talks, there is rarely, if ever, the emotional pain experienced in a divorce. This means that the detachment practiced by the labor mediator is not as easily achieved by the divorce mediator. An increase of a nickel an hour or a complicated contract clause does not involve the mediator in the same way as does rejection, child visitation rights, and similar issues.

Labor talks may be used to play out other issues—such as the image a company director wants to develop to impress the stockholders or the efforts of a union negotiator who wants to run for election—which can lead to an unrealistically tough position by either side. Divorce talks can be used to relive the breakdown of the marriage or, indeed, attempt to prevent its dissolution.

The divorce mediator is aware of that pain and needs to develop a theory of divorce in which to practice mediation. For it is clear now that divorce mediation must involve an understanding of the divorce process and of the emotional stages. When the mediator has a theoretical position regarding divorce, the mediation process can be used to enhance the process of adjustment to divorce.

It is commonly agreed that most growth is accompanied by pain. Or, in other words, emotional pain and its causes can be used to enable the pained individual to grow. However, pain does not automatically assure growth. It is possible for people to stagnate in a pool of pain that effectively handicaps them for the rest of their lives. The mediator assists in assuring that there is growth from this painful process; it begins when s/he identifies the pain and anger surrounding the divorce and legitimizes it.

Following that the mediator explores the power relationships and how that power is symbolized within the marriage. The parties can usually identify the pain that came from this unequal power and perhaps even see that the pain was often caused by the limitations imposed on one person by the other's power. As this happens the rejected party is assisted in understanding the possibilities that are opened up by a mutual divorce rather than a unilateral one.

Once both parties want to dissolve the marriage because it is in each of their best interests to do so, the leaving party's power over the rejected party is limited because the rejection is now more mutual. If, at the same time, there is a sharing of knowledge of finances, then there is also a sharing of power. When, as is often the case, the husband is both the rejecting partner and the finance controller, then as the mutual rejection and shared knowledge of finances takes hold, the wife begins to assume a more equal power relationship, which results in a more mutually satisfactory settlement.

During the first few sessions the mediator should be constantly alert for signals of unreadiness. Care must be taken not to confuse misunderstanding or uncertainty about the mediation process with a reluctance to enter into it. The stress of divorce, which impairs the clients' ability to focus clearly, may appear as reluctance. The mediator will separate resistance from misunderstanding by repeating important pieces of information so that the clients fully understand what is happening.

In the case of Bea and Ben, the first few sessions were difficult because Bea often seemed preoccupied and not always to be following the discussion. She complained that this was due to the pressures of business, but it was also probably caused by the stress of the divorce and the newness of the mediation process at a time when she was under pressure at work. She eased up as the mediation process unfolded and understood that I was willing to slow down to her pace.

In another case a couple were referred to me and, from the report of the referring therapist, I did not believe they were ready for divorce. The wife appeared willing, but the husband did not seem to be ready. When I set the fee at $18 a session on the basis on his take-home pay of $350 a week, he objected violently, claiming that he had so many debts that he could not pay the fee. The therapist asked if I would reduce it. I refused because I decided that if the couple really wanted to enter into a formal separation and subsequent divorce, the husband should be willing to pay a reasonable amount. I did not take them as clients and terminated the session with a statement of willingness to be available should they change their minds.

Following that session, the therapist observed that she had sensed a great feeling of relief on the husband's part at the thought that he could avoid mediation by refusing to pay the fee, because she had not thought that he really wanted the divorce. She admitted that she had reached a point where she did not know what to do with the clients and had hoped that sending them to me would solve the problem. But, while I was willing to be their mediator, they were not ready for separation or divorce.

chapter 5

Implementing
the model

Divorce mediation does not follow the pattern of a fifty-minute hour. Although I discuss this process in terms of sessions, a session may last from one to five hours, depending on the stage of the negotiations and the characteristics of the couple. Therefore I do not schedule more than one couple in an evening. The mediator needs great time flexibility to be able to take as much time as the couple need to make a move in that particular encounter.

The process usually begins with a session of one hour. However, subsequent sessions usually run at least one-and-one-half hours. When the mediator is seeing each party separately, these separate sessions cannot be crammed into a short space of time. Finally, when the couple are trading in the later sessions, the mediator keeps them at the bargaining table for as long as a give and take is happening. To break a good trading session because of arbitrary time limits would destroy the effectiveness of mediation. Therefore, in reading descriptions of the sessions, the reader should bear in mind that they often consist of long periods of time and sometimes continue over a week or two.

The first session

The first session is a difficult one, because the mediator must attempt to achieve a number of goals. S/he must establish the mediator's credibility and set the tone for the subsequent relationship, while explaining the process, clarifying the clients' expectations, and establishing empathy with them. At the same time s/he must determine whether they are really ready for mediation.

The mediator should attempt upon entering the room to establish the tone for an informal, trusting relationship. Introductions should be on a first-name basis (Satir, 1975, p. 200) and the seating arrangements as non-hierarchical as possible. Use of a table to separate the mediator from the couple should be avoided. The best seating arrangement is a triangle of chairs, with each person facing the other two. This will help ease some of the early tension.

The mediator must then move immediately to establish credibility. This involves being very clear about the process and helping the couple understand the mediator's role and how it will work. My opening gambit is usually as follows:

"More and more people are getting divorced today, and they want to do it without tearing one another apart. Of course, there is a lot of anger and pain involved in separating; I understand that and won't try to hide it. However, it doesn't mean that we have to view each other as adversaries. The divorce mediation process allows you to negotiate your own separation agreement. You put into the agreement only what you want in it. That means that when you have gone through the process of negotiating, of giving and taking, you will have an agreement in writing that belongs to you.

"Now, during the negotiations, I will help you identify the major issues that need negotiating. I will help each of you to prepare your positions. In this way I will be able to tell you whether something you want is within normal bounds.

"I won't be able to impose anything on you. I have no legal authority and cannot arbitrate. I will not decide for you. I will help you decide for yourselves.

"In the beginning of the discussions we will start out all three together. Then I will spend time with each of you individually. At times we will come together as a trio; at other times we will meet separately.

"There may be times when you want to raise an idea but you're not quite sure how it will sound to the other party. Well, you can use me to try out those ideas to see whether they will fly. At times I will shuttle between the two of you, suggesting compromises, carrying ideas, but all the time working for a good settlement.

"Because, you see, my commitment is not to either of you but to the settlement. I will work for each of you individually and both of you jointly to reach the settlement.

"There may be occasions when I spend a long time with one of you and only a short time with the other. This does not mean that one is more important or needy than the other. It merely means that I need that time to help *you* get the settlement.

"We will start out today with a regular one-hour session. After that we will schedule time as we need it. I find from experience that it is best to schedule a few hours in the evening—the reason why I only take one couple per evening is to have the time they require. Then we might drop back to a one-hour session and, as we come close to an agreement, we might meet for a few hours on a weekend or at some other convenient date.

"I am going to give you some materials this evening that describe the process step by step. (See Appendix A.) You don't have to read it now. Take it home and read it at your leisure.

"I'm sure you have many questions about the process and me, so why don't we start with those?"

Function of the monologue

In this monologue I have tried to establish a number of things. I have described mediation in a way that establishes my credibility. I have established my authority as a mediator and have helped set the tone for the subsequent negotiations. I have explained to the couple that this is a system that works in a way they can understand, thereby clarifying their expectations. Finally, I have established a beginning empathy with them by a careful, nonjudgmental description of the process and by reminding them that they are not alone in the decision to divorce. I have also recognized their right to and the legitimacy of their anger and the meaning of their pain. I hope to have begun to establish a trusting relationship with them.

Much of the purpose of the monologue is reinforced in the question and answer period that follows this initial presentation. There is often confusion about the role of the mediator. One of the clients will usually inquire whether I am a lawyer or ask a similar question to determine my professional credentials. The couple will want to know the interface between the mediator and the lawyer. They will be interested about what power I have over them. It is important, therefore, to underscore the fact that the mediator cannot impose a settlement and that either party is free to walk out of the mediation at any time.

In the give and take that follows, clients are usually anxious to begin trying out ideas with the mediator as to what is fair or what is right. The wife will often explore how mediation compares to an adversarial legal proceeding. She might want to use the latter as a bargaining threat to the husband: "I know the judge will give me everything if you don't agree here."

There is a danger that the mediator will be drawn into providing answers to the couple that define the terms of the settlement. S/he should carefully avoid that. The mediator is not there to tell the couple who is right or what is wrong. S/he is there to mediate a settlement that must belong to the couple.

This fact needs to be reinforced by emphasizing the joint ownership of the agreement they are about to negotiate. The couple can be reminded that they may go to court at any time but that each must be prepared to accept the vagaries of the legal system because, in court, the judge is the final arbiter whereas, in mediation, they are.

Collecting basic data

When the questions have been answered the mediator begins to collect the basic data. The Intake Interview Form reproduced in Figure 5–1 provides the mediator with needed data, together with indications about how the characteristics of the couple will affect the mediation process.

Asking the clients separately for their addresses achieves two goals. First, asking any couple for joint information will usually bring a response from the dominant party or the family spokesperson. Asking the other party the same information recognizes that person's identity and demonstrates the mediator's neutrality. In addition, by asking for the addresses rather than, "Are you living together?" the mediator gets a response to both questions.

If the couple are still living together, the mediator will want to explore the nature of the current living arrangements. This information will indicate the couple's position on the Divorce Adjustment Process scale and can provide another indicator of whether they are ready for divorce. A couple that continue to share a bed and maintain conjugal relations are unlikely to be ready to make the physical and emotional break necessary to separate. They are probably looking for marriage counseling.

The date and site of the marriage will be needed later when the final agreement is drafted, as will data on the children. Obtaining it now will give the mediator a brief family profile and help define the scope of the negotiations to follow.

The referral source is a necessary part of the records, whereas the question as to who initiated the divorce and whether the other party opposed it will help forecast the couple's behavior in mediation.

For example, when one party initiates the divorce and the other opposes it, it indicates that the rejection issue may loom large for the noninitiator. The mediator will need to watch for the guilt syndrome in the initiator and for lack of self-worth in the rejected with its accompanying anger.

By asking whether the decision to divorce was gradual or sudden, the mediator also gets the couple to talk about some of the causes of the divorce. In the event the decision to divorce is recent and sudden, the mediator might want to explore whether the couple is ready for mediation. They may really want marriage counseling and help to avoid divorce.

The question relating to whether they are in therapy now will elicit

DIVORCE MEDIATION INTAKE INTERVIEW

	Male	Female
Name		
Address		
Phone		
Occupation		

Current living arrangements
if still residing together.

Marriage Date _____

Place - County & State _____

Children

Name	Date of Birth

What do you know about divorce mediation?

Referral

Who initiated the divorce?

Did other oppose it?

Was decision gradual or sudden?

In therapy now?

What are your main goals in a settlement?

Figure 5–1. Divorce mediation intake interview form.

the information as to whether they have been in therapy, jointly or individually, and if they are not in therapy at that moment, this will alert the mediator that s/he will have to carry some of the therapist's role in the mediation process. There is no way of avoiding some therapeutic function, and indeed, I believe it is helpful, provided the mediator understands the dangers of entering into a therapeutic relationship with the couple. The time-out concept permits a discrete separation of the roles.

Finally, the question, "What are your main goals in a settlement?" focuses the session on the purpose of mediation and helps the mediator get a feel for how each partner views the process and how the negotiations might proceed.

At this point the mediator can move in two ways. If the couple have not thought through the financial consequences of two separate households and it appears that little discussion about this has preceded the couple's visit, then s/he will refer them to the Budgeting Section of the materials (see Appendix A).

Budgeting materials

My experience is that very few couples use all of the budgeting materials. However, it is helpful for the woman if she has no previous experience handling the finances. By giving a highly structured approach to the problem, the mediator makes it less frightening for someone who has not budgeted before. On the other hand, where the husband proposes moving out, an evening's work on the budget developing what it will cost to live alone will prove helpful in setting more realistic parameters to the bargaining.

The materials given to the clients really have two purposes. The main one is to involve them in the process by having them understand each step; the other is to define a set of tasks that must be accomplished in order to reach a settlement. To focus on these simple, step-by-step tasks is therapeutic for people under stress from the emotional devastation wrought by the decision to divorce.

Some couples will bring the materials to each session. Others will take them and lose them or never indicate they have them. Their use during the actual negotiations is not as important as their value in helping establish the mediator's credibility and helping couples focus their range of divorce emotions into separation tasks.

The first session usually concludes with the mediator assuring the couple that s/he is available at any time during the week to answer any questions they may have about the process or to clarify any issues. S/he then indicates that the second session will be split in two and that s/he will see each of them separately for the Individual Interview and the beginning of goal setting. While this is the focus of the second session, it is also the primary opportunity for the mediator to assess the power relationships of the couple. Thus each step of the Individual Interview and the separate goal-setting dialogues has a stated and an unstated purpose.

The second session

The stated purpose of the second session is to continue building the family profile through the Individual Interview form reproduced as Figure 5–2 (see p. 64), and to begin developing individual goals. The unstated purpose is to assess the likelihood of success by determining the couple's power relationships and how these will affect the actual negotiations. Separate rooms are needed for this determination.

This session will provide the mediator with the majority of clues as to the likelihood of successful mediation. If the couple return without having done any of the assigned tasks, it could indicate that they are not ready to go through with the divorce. It could also mean that they do not have or know how to get the data or that one of them has the information but is trying to hide it.

If only one party comes empty-handed, the mediator spends time going over the budget helping him or her understand it and fill it out. While this is happening, the mediator learns whether the individual inactivity is due to an unwillingness, a lack of knowledge, or a strategy.

The wife often does not have access to the desired information. The husband often does not complete the budget sheets because he does not want to divulge all of the data. Since knowledge is power, few husbands who have controlled the budget during the marriage are willing to share that knowledge (power) with the spouse—at least not in the early part of the negotiations. One of the functions of the mediator is to begin that sharing process.

The mediator will have to confront the party who is deliberately withholding the information. The confrontation takes place in the private, not the joint, session. The mediator points out that all of the cards must be on the table if real negotiations are to take place.

If the power relationship is unequal in the beginning, attempts to equalize it will assist the process of negotiations. The equalization is important because negotiations cannot take place between two relatively unequal parties. If too much power is on one side, that side will impose the terms of the settlement on the other. The degree to which actual negotiations take place depends on the perception that each party has about the relative power that can be exercised by the other. This equalization can take place during the mediation process through a sharing of knowledge and through the development of individual strengths that limit the other's power.

As I assist the woman to break out of this isolation by helping her to understand some of the budgeting issues and by developing alternative sources of support, I am also helping to equalize the power relationship to enable the negotiations to begin.

Thus I would argue that helping to identify weaknesses in either party and helping that party deal with those weaknesses is helping both parties and maintaining the mediator's commitment to the settlement. For without a relative equalization, negotiations are not possible.

This is another area in which divorce mediation differs sharply from labor mediation. A labor mediator makes no attempt to alter the balance of power between a union and an employer. S/he assesses the power relationship and often uses the differential to pressure the weaker party into a settlement. The labor mediator cannot move to equalize the power relationship because to do so would be politically unwise.

Another important difference is that in a labor mediation a temporary conflict is being mediated between two permanent institutions. The union and the company will continue to exist in relatively the same relationship after the contract dispute has been settled. Divorce mediation, however, is a stage in the dissolution of an institutional relationship. The husband and wife will be unrelated after the divorce. The mediator will not expect to be called back three or five years later to mediate another temporary conflict. Divorce, by and large, is permanent.

The exception to this is where a divorced couple remain entangled through a continuing battle over the children. The process described here is also valid in post-divorce situations involving custody.

Individual interviews

In these interviews the mediator completes the Individual Interview form shown in Figure 5–2. The purpose of these questions is to help the mediator determine the individual strength of each of the parties as distinct from the power relationship.

By asking for their view of the reasons for the divorce, s/he can begin to assess who is the rejected party and the extent to which each person blames him/herself rather than the other. Obviously this will, in some way, influence the couple's individual behavior during the negotiations.

In exploring responses to the question, "What other relationships do you have?" the mediator can find out whether the client has any close

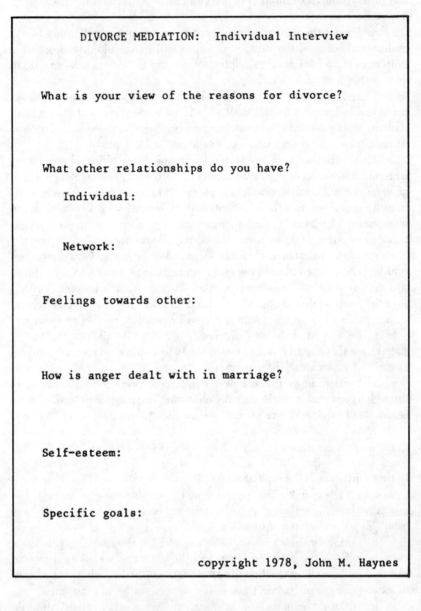

```
        DIVORCE MEDIATION:   Individual Interview


What is your view of the reasons for divorce?


What other relationships do you have?
   Individual:


   Network:


Feelings towards other:


How is anger dealt with in marriage?


Self-esteem:


Specific goals:


                        copyright 1978, John M. Haynes
```

Figure 5–2. Divorce mediation: individual interview.

friends to support her/him during the process and whether the person is plugged into any network. For example, if the wife has no friends outside the family, does not belong to any organization or group, and has no apparent network, her problems are going to be complicated. The mediator can explore ways in which s/he might plug the wife into an appropriate network to help provide her with emotional resources independent of the husband.

Identification of a local women's group and suggestions on how she might gain an introduction could lead to that group's helping her find a sense of her own identity and providing such material benefits as learning to drive and sharing babysitters, experiences, and frustrations. This action would add to the power of the wife.

The next set of questions helps the mediator gain a sense of how the negotiations will proceed. "Feelings toward other" will indicate the depth of anger. Does she really want to take him for all he is worth? Does he really intend to walk out without meeting his obligations to the spouse and children? The depth of the feelings identified here will give the mediator a sense of what to expect in the talks. These private expressions of feelings about the other can also be used to measure the "public" response to the other in the joint sessions. It is important for the mediator to be able to distinguish between posture and real feelings.

Legitimating feelings

An expression of deep animosity during the private talks might not be matched by similar strong feelings in the joint talks. Yet if the mediator does not work to bring the anger out in an appropriate way, the real issue causing the anger may stay submerged but still strong enough to block a settlement.

In this case the mediator would want to legitimate this anger and help get it onto the bargaining table so that its cause can be understood and dealt with by both parties. The experience with Dan and Cindy demonstrates this problem.

Cindy was angry with Dan because of what she felt was his rejection of their handicapped daughter. On the other hand, Cindy was also angry that Dan wanted open visitation rights and had dropped in unannounced a number of times at odd hours. But she could not deal with the visitation situation until she dealt with the rejection issue. A failure to deal with the rejection issue would prevent her from coming to an agreement on the rest of the terms, which were comparatively generous.

Getting Cindy to discuss her anger at Dan's rejection of the daughter in a private session helped me to get both of them to discuss this issue in one of the joint sessions. Once she had expressed this anger at Dan, Cindy was able to raise the issue of visitation and define when Dan could drop by the apartment. These two items were dealt with at the same session and led to a general agreement on all of the other issues involved in the separation agreement.

In the discussion on the Divorce Adjustment Process I pointed out that anger was often a secondary emotional response to a more primary feeling. In this case Cindy was responding to her feelings of victimization at being left with the full burden of caring for the handicapped daughter and to her feelings of loss of the marriage relationship. Although these feelings were not dealt with therapeutically during mediation, the act of bringing them to the surface and dealing with them as one of the issues to be negotiated became therapeutic.

In contrast, the sentiment of real warmth toward the other party might not be carried over to the joint session. In that case the mediator would know that even while the couple were hostile toward one another when they were together, sufficient "good" feelings remained for the mediator to use as the bridge between the two positions at a later crucial stage of the negotiations.

It is useful for the mediator to know the answer to "How is anger dealt with in the marriage?" because whichever way it is dealt with, it will be dealt with similarly in mediation.

The mediator does not ask the clients about their "self-esteem"; this is determined by talking about the other questions. However, self-esteem is an important ingredient in negotiations, and if one party has low self-esteem s/he will also have a limited sense of power. Often this low self-esteem is fostered by the other party and knowing how that is done will help the mediator counter it in ways that help build self-esteem. This is usually done through connecting the party with an appropriate network.

In one case the husband had low self-esteem. He had no friends outside the family and no way of developing them. His wife initiated the divorce and fed his low self-esteem by constantly telling him that one of the main reasons she was leaving him was because he was an old stay-at-home without any outside interests. She then used his low self-esteem to persuade him to propose an overly generous settlement that would be very difficult for him to maintain and would lock him into not being able to go out simply because he had no money.

In the discussions with the husband I learned of his interest in movies and art. I connected him with the local community cinema group, which gave him the opportunity to begin to develop an independent network. It also gave him grounds for rejecting the one-sided settlement proposed by his wife. He now had a claim to the car and some additional money to be able to get out and develop his interests. At that point the real negotiations began.

Goal setting

The couple are now ready to begin setting their goals. In the first few sessions I help identify the goals that are major to each party and those that are less important. I compare the two separate sets of goals to see which items have a high disagreement component and which a low one. Finally I watch to see whether there is any difference in the importance of a goal, or the strength with which it is held, in the individual sessions compared to the joint sessions.

During the first session, as part of the intake process, I ask, "What are your goals in mediation?" This usually elicits a hesitant response when both parties talk about wanting to get an agreement. I then rephrase the question, "What do you think are going to be the major areas of disagreement?" The response to this question usually indicates areas the couple have already argued about. The man usually responds that alimony and child support are big issues. The woman usually agrees and adds visitation as an important item for her.

In the individual discussions of the second session I probe these goals more deeply. I try to avoid specifics, such as how much alimony, in the early sessions, since I do not want to block development of the total picture or an understanding of the relationship between the pieces. Once the broad picture has been painted, I try to find out what long-term goals each party has for her/himself.

I ask, "What do you want out of this divorce?" This is always a difficult question to answer. Clients usually begin by saying they want what is fair for the spouse or the children. In every case the initial response has been to claim to want to take care of the other person. He wants to take care of her; she does not want to leave him threadbare. Both want what is best for the children.

I begin to push them, asking, "But what do *you* want?" I rephrase it again, asking, "But when the money and custody issues are settled, what do *you* want for *yourself* out of this divorce?" As the clients begin to feel comfortable in identifying their own real needs, they also begin to think about the post-divorce period and what they want. Thus, I have helped them bridge the immediate litigation-transition period and the later re-direction period by identifying goals that can be begun now but will be completed in the future.

An example of this situation might be that the wife wants to remarry as soon as possible. The cause of the divorce is the relationship with the other man. In that case her major goal is to remarry. Although she cannot make this goal an item in the separation agreement, it will constantly affect the negotiations. I note these goals to help me understand some of the dynamics and possible compromises that will arise in the actual negotiations.

Frequently I find that one or both parties have difficulty in thinking about what they need without defining it by what the other party can or cannot do. Most people seem to experience difficulty asking for things for themselves. They also have difficulty breaking out of patterns of relationships that may have existed for many years.

During the individual sessions in which I assist each party to define goals, I find that an important role for the mediator is to legitimate the right of either party to have goals or demands that the other should recognize.

Articulating hidden agendas

By articulating these unmet needs, the subsequent divorce adjustment is truncated because the mediation process not only dissolves the marriage but does it in a way that opens up the redirection period possibilities immediately. Without identifying the unmet needs of both parties, the negotiations would probably revolve solely around money and custody, with no serious thought being given to the way in which the money and custody issues affect the personal goals of the two parties.

I use the information gleaned from the individual goal-setting sessions during the later give-and-take negotiations. I remind the parties of their other goals and that the way they negotiate about money, for example, will affect the realization of their own goals.

Thus I help people keep their own real self-interest uppermost in the negotiations. This facilitates the process and helps the couple come out of the negotiations with more than a dollars-and-cents division of the marriage assets.

The individual goal-setting sessions have another purpose. They permit me to compare the private positions of the two parties. Often those private discussions reveal that there is no conflict on a given item, even though one or both of the parties may feel there is. In that case I plan to get that item onto the table early in the negotiations, because it is a "high-success" item that can be built upon to achieve subsequent success on more difficult items.

On the other hand, the private sessions sometimes reveal that there is a serious difference on an item that, when the couple are together, appears to be easily solved. This is the case when one party is afraid of the other and does not have the courage to raise an issue even though there is serious disagreement. I also note this and determine ways of bringing the disagreement into the open, usually by articulating the concern as the neutral third party. Once it is in the open, the disagreement can be dealt with directly by the two parties.

When I raise a contentious issue, I am doing so within the context of the power relationships of the couple. The mediator needs to intervene in this area to help achieve a balance of power that permits an open discussion of the submerged issue. For if the fear remains submerged, the other party maintains an element of additional power over the spouse, Placing the issue on the table causes it to be dealt with; the fear diminishes and power is equalized.

Developing a family profile

Finally, I use the early sessions to develop a profile of the family. Obviously, the number and ages of the children will have a significant impact on the negotiations. When there are young children involved, the issues of custody, visitation, and access will be intertwined with the amount of child support.

I am interested in gaining each party's perception of their relationship to the children and their goals regarding them. In the process I begin to lay the groundwork for the parents to understand that they will always be parents, even though they are moving to end their status as husband and wife.

Parent reaction to the ideas developed in the chapter on children (Chapter 3) will indicate to me how consonant their views and attitudes are with mine about access and involvement.

The mediator is now ready to begin negotiations. In order to do this s/he has already compiled an inventory of:

1. basic data and current living arrangements,
2. who initiated the divorce and response of the other,
3. the strength of each party's relationships outside the marriage,
4. the relative position of each party within a broad network,
5. a sense of the feelings toward the other,
6. an understanding of how anger is dealt with in the marriage and therefore likely to appear in mediation,
7. an estimate of the self-esteem of each party,
8. an assessment of the power relationships within the marriage,
9. the main goals of each party (shared with other),
10. the specific goals of each party (not shared with other),
11. a profile of the family and the relationships with the children.

From this inventory the mediator has developed:

1. an identification of the commonly agreed issues with which to open negotiations,
2. a sense of those items each wants from the dissolution that have not been articulated but which help redirect toward the future,
3. a strategy for power equalization.

The parties can now come together for the first joint discussion of substantive issues.

Negotiating

In their book *The Social Psychology of Bargaining*, Morley and Stephenson state that in negotiating, the parties to a dispute establish the terms on which they are willing to cooperate (1977, p. 15). By selecting divorce mediation rather than the adversarial legal route, couples have made the decision to cooperate in resolving their conflicting aims.

The same authors conducted a literature search, which I shall use in defining some of the terms used in this section (1977, pp. 23–24). Their search indicates a certain amount of common agreement on four major components to the process of negotiating. First, they believe that the negotiators must engage in some joint decision making. In doing so they move beyond a conflict of opinion or interests to an attempt to resolve the conflict.

Second, each participant in a negotiation has some mixed motives. In divorce, couples want to reach an agreement on the various joint actions that need to be taken. However, they also have an investment in the emotional relationships that led to the divorce.

Third, each party has a different set of preferences or order of priority concerning the same set of items. Deciding which to pursue requires some strategic decision making by both parties. It is this concept that leads to the trading that I will discuss later.

Finally, negotiating involves talking about a relationship before doing anything about it. In labor and management relations the discussion usually centers on the symbiotic nature of the relationship. In divorce it demands that the couple talk about the decision to end the relationship of husband and wife.

Negotiation then is defined in general terms as the process of determining what form of joint action the two parties might take to resolve or handle the dispute between them. Bargaining therefore is the process of negotiating for an agreement which involves some give and take, compromise, and redefinition of the issues by both sides.

Most of the research on negotiations deals with organizations or situations such as labor–management talks, business price bargaining, or international diplomacy. Some work though, deals with individual relationships (Scanzoni, 1972). The problem facing the mediator, however, is that divorce mediation, unlike other negotiations, deals with two neophytes. The couple have no experience in formal bargaining and therefore need a framework in which to act.

To provide that framework is the main purpose of the material I give to clients (see Appendix A). I spend time with both parties helping develop a sense of the process of negotiations, the tactics of bargaining, and the skills to articulate the latter at the table. Although most of the clients read the material, I spend time reinforcing these ideas by helping each of the parties refine their skills, hopefully at an equal level, so as to facilitate the process of give and take that is essential to a final agreement.

Reviewing progress

At the next session when we three meet together, I begin by reviewing the common items discussed at each of the private sessions. I identify the areas of agreement or those close to agreement and suggest that the session begin with a discussion of those items.

The review of items discussed in the private sessions has two purposes. The first is to get a list onto the table that will meet with a minimum of disagreement, the second to give each party some information about what happened in the other's private session.

Let us examine these two areas, taking the latter first. Most people are apprehensive about the individual sessions. They are not sure about what the spouse told the mediator while they were not there. "Did the spouse reveal something unpleasant about me?" "Is there some secret strategy that was developed without me?" "Did the mediator favor the spouse rather than me?" All of these fears can be lessened if the mediator spends a little time sharing with both parties what happened in each of the individual sessions.

Obviously the mediator cannot reveal any confidential information. S/he cannot indicate any bargaining positions that were suggested in the sessions. S/he cannot reveal any personal information that was learned in private. S/he can, however, review the common items on which there is agreement or near agreement, thus showing both parties that s/he dealt with the other in much the same way.

As the mediator lists, for example, the couple's general agreement about the house, s/he demonstrates to each of them together that s/he and the other partner talked about the same things in the same way when they were separate. This tends to reduce the anxiety about what goes on in private sessions and helps clear the air during the joint sessions for more productive talks.

The other reason for getting the list of low-disagreement items on the table is to set the tone for the negotiations. Clearly, if the first joint negotiating session is productive because the items chosen for discussion were not particularly contentious, the confidence of the parties in the process is increased. By starting out with the smallest, simplest items and helping the couple achieve success by agreeing on them, the mediator helps build the confidence of the couple to deal with the more difficult items.

The couple are unlikely to come to mediation from a marriage marked by successful cooperation. They will be skeptical of success because their marriage is probably a series of failures to cooperate (Deutsch, 1969, p. 27).

Building on each small success, the mediator moves toward the more contentious areas of disagreement. In the process s/he demonstrates to the couple that they can indeed reach an agreement about things. The mediator builds those skills of conflict resolution slowly and surely through demonstration rather than talk.

Some items will not need lengthy discussion. If I have determined that the couple have already agreed to certain items, I begin by defining these. I indicate that both parties seem to be in agreement on them and, once gaining their assent, place them on the list of agreed items.

Gaining accommodations

As the session goes on, I slowly add to the list those items about which there is a minor disagreement. They will be placed on the table one at a time in a preselected way. In the private sessions I have determined which of these low-disagreement items mean most and least to each of the parties. I place one on the table that requires a minor accommodation from the wife. Having achieved that, I take an item requiring a minor accommodation from the husband. Usually, if the first spouse has made an accommodation, the other spouse will follow and make an accommodation on his/her item.

This act of cooperative accommodation is usually well received by both parties, and I continue to build a sense of mutual trust in the process. The first joint session is generally confined to items upon which there will not be a major disagreement. In the event an item turns out to be more contentious than projected, I simply remove it from the table with the comment that "we will return to it later." Since few people are anxious to pursue conflict, both parties usually agree to its temporary removal.

It is not essential to reach agreement on all of the items at that session. Indeed, it is possible that no items will have been formally agreed upon at the end of the session. If one of the parties is hesitant about a specific item, I do not push that party for a statement then and there. I am careful to prevent one spouse from pressuring the other to agree to an item. The mediator must be sure that the areas of agreement are real and that both parties are comfortable with them. If there is any sense of discomfort by either party, the mediator moves to shield that person from premature decision making by postponing the item for further consideration. This gives the spouse time to think it through, discuss it with a friend, or examine it further privately with the mediator.

After that joint session I review my notes of the process and check for any reaction or behavior that differed substantially from the feelings expressed in the private session. There is no reason to suppose that everything the client tells me in the private session is, in fact, based on reality. The chemistry or response of the spouse to a specific point may make an item that appeared simple in private very difficult in the joint sessions.

For example, disposition of personal property has not proven to be difficult. Most couples have a fairly clear idea about how they will split the household furnishings. In the individual sessions they might each indicate similar lists of what they want. However, in the joint session, one spouse may describe an item as "that thing your sister gave us," which could trigger off pent-up hostility about the way the spouse has treated the other's family.

I will not necessarily have picked up this family feud in the individual sessions. However, as it comes pouring out in the joint session, I give it a reasonable time to ventilate before removing the item from the table, pending further thought.[1]

My task is to rebuild an atmosphere of give and take. This is done by reviewing those items that have already been agreed on and then moving to another item that appears to have a low-disagreement factor.

---

[1]"Since the Family Law Act of 1970 created the 'no fault' divorce, many of these people never got a chance to have their 'day in court' and tell their story. They are frustrated and they need a trained person to listen to them" (Saurez, Weston, & Hartstein, 1978, p. 279).

Learning to trade

Many couples have trouble understanding and accepting "trading." They often think it is wrong to trade one agreement for another. This appears to be part of the earlier problem of not being able to identify their own real needs. Therefore, the mediator helps each of the parties become comfortable with trading.

As the initial lists are being prepared, I ask the client, "What would happen if you asked him for a in return for b?" The initial response is usually, "Oh, I can't do that; it's not right." Or the party will respond emotionally, "Why should I give a? I'm entitled to b and should get it anyway."

This begins the process of explaining the legitimacy of offering concessions in return for other concessions. I compare it to labor bargaining and encourage the clients to try out some trading on small items. If the emotional response is maintained by either client, I begin to ask them whether they want to negotiate an agreement or win a fight. I explore with them the consequences of taking a position that one must get something because it is one's "right"; I explain that the result will be two implacable foes, each wanting what is his/her right and neither understanding that the way to get that right is to recognize the other's.

The actual bargaining part of the negotiations rarely lasts long. It appears that there is a need for considerable preparation time before the one or two sessions in which the actual agreement is hammered out.

At these bargaining sessions I do a lot of shuttling back and forth. Having defined the areas of disagreement, I help each of the clients prepare different responses to them. I try out with one party a proposal that involves some compromise. Checking his/her response, I try out the same package with the other party. In the process the second party may make some amendments to the proposal, which I take back and try out with the first party. I slowly add items to the proposal, until we have a package that includes all of the substantive areas of disagreement. Some of the items can be agreed upon as a result of redefining the issue; we gain agreement on others by trade-off and on another few by unilateral compromise.

As we move toward the final agreement, I try to hold all of the major items open so that we can reach an agreement on the total package. In this way I avoid leaving one item open at the end upon which we cannot get agreement, because all of the compromsing and trading took place on the earlier items.

In my experience mediating divorces, I find that the final agreement often revolves around two items and that both items are important to both parties. When mediation reaches that point I usually suggest to each of the partners that they consider each taking one of the items. I leave them to select which one. They usually have a good idea what each of the issues means to the other and can make a selection quickly.

The Ben and Bea case is a good example of the trading process. Ben wanted to limit the alimony/child support. Bea wanted an assurance that she could survive the first couple of years on her own. When I met with Bea I asked her how long she thought she would need the higher support payments. She said she thought they would be important for the next three years. I asked her how she would feel about linking the support to the fifteen-year-old daughter's maintenance, thus giving it a time frame. (Child support usually ends when the child reaches the age of 18 in most states unless the agreement provides otherwise.) She thought that would be a good idea.

Then I met with Ben and asked him whether his concern was over paying any support for the child or over the open-endedness of the alimony. He thought it was the latter and agreed that he would be wlling to pay higher child support over the next three years rather than pay for lifelong alimony. We discussed the tax consequences of this for him and he thought he would pay all the money in child support, even if it increased the tax liability of the family.

Next I discussed with Bea the possibility of her taking all of the support monies as child support and waiving alimony entirely. She said that if she could get enough in child support she could agree. Thus I first had each of them agree to the principle that all of the support should be in child support, and that it would be a greater amount than had been discussed earlier.

Once I had agreement in principle, I explored the actual amounts. At this point I shuttled back and forth between the two parties, working out precise figures. As we came close to an agreement on the amounts, I added the other issues to the package and at the end of three hours had the couple signing the agreement.

I find that the mediator's role in the bargaining sessions is to

1. help the couple define which items can be modified, traded, or dropped,
2. listen to both positions carefully to detect any messages that one is sending to the other and make sure that the other party also picks up on those messages,
3. take ideas back and forth in a way that does not commit either party to a specific proposal. Clients are able to be more creative in their thinking if they know that every idea will not be immediately incorporated into the agreement,

4. suggest different ways to put a satisfactory agreement together. Clients often need help in thinking about how to reshape the package,
5. define what is reasonable. There are times when I have to intervene to tell clients that the proposal they are making is unreasonable; I tell them that it is outside the norm or that I doubt the idea will fly, and persuade them to modify their position,
6. keep track of agreements as they are reached so as to be able to show what still needs to be done. This does not imply that an agreement on one issue cannot be reopened later as a way of gaining agreement on other issues, but it is helpful for the mediator to remove agreed-upon items from the discussion to continue focusing down on the remaining items,
7. help the couple reach a conclusion. I find that I usually have to initiate the last trade-off or compromise that leads to the final package.

When the final package is agreed upon, there appears to be a need for some kind of ceremony to indicate the end. I usually bring out a bottle to give the participants a symbolic way of closing the mediation process and to toast the new beginning.

Using other professionals

At times special conditions arise that call for an outside expert. In proposing the model I suggested that the mediator would call on the advice of an accountant, lawyer, or therapist. In practice I found that this disempowered the clients. It is much more useful to refer the clients to the outside expert so that they have the advice needed to shape their response to a specific point.

In the Milt and Jane case in Chapter 6, an issue arose as to how to apportion the support Milt was paying. How much should go to child support and how much to alimony? There are important tax considerations in the actual choice. However, instead of providing the answer, I suggested that they consult with their accountant and get the advice. This slowed down the process because we had to wait for the accountant to respond, but both parties felt more in control of the process as a result. In addition, it lessened my responsibilities and kept me as the mediator instead of turning me into the all-around expert.

As the clients bring back the expert advice and shape the agreement, we begin to talk about how the written document is going to be prepared. I draft the document, based on my notes, and send it to the couple about a week later. They review the agreement and each suggests changes based on higher recollection. I verify the changes with the other party and, if there is general agreement, revise the document.

Once the document is revised to the satisfaction of both parties, each of them takes it to an attorney, who reviews it with her/him. If the attorneys suggest any changes, I become involved again and revise the document once more until it is ready to be signed and used as the basis of a formal separation agreement that can be filed with the court.

Not all cases end in an agreement. Not all couples are ready for mediation. In the next chapter I describe nine cases, most of which ended in agreement. Each case had its own unique aspects. Two cases were terminated by me on the grounds that the couple either did not want to divorce or were not able to use mediation. One case is still in progress and illustrates how some cases can be suspended while the parties determine what course of action they really want to take.

The cases also illustrate many of the points discussed in the first five chapters and will help the reader understand the dynamics of the general principles when applied to specific situations.

Testing model assumptions

In developing the model of divorce mediation, I assumed that separating the symbolic demands from the substantive ones would be a problem for the mediator. In practice this has not proven to be so. Couples have not had symbolic issues to wave before one another. Rather, the only time an issue was used for a secondary purpose was in the case of Marvin and Sheila.

In that case the husband used the custody issue to try to avoid paying alimony or reasonable support. However, even when used as a "cover," it is still a substantive issue. In this instance I had to find a way of sidetracking the item to allow us to proceed to the negotiable issues. My feeling was that if we placed the custody issue aside with the promise to deal with it at some later date, and if we could resolve the financial support issue, the custody question would cease to exist.

There are a number of ways of placing an item on "hold," and the way chosen by Marvin reflected his style. However, the danger of postponement is that the mediator will end the negotiations with an unresolved substantive issue that does not lend itself to trading. The task of the mediator is to remove unreasonable roadblocks (once it is clear they are unreasonable) in the expectation that resolution of other issues will resolve the removed item.

Symbolic issues are probably lacking in divorce because the couple, unlike union and management, are not playing to a wider constituency. Symbolic demands raised by a union or management representative are designed to impress the shareholders or the rank and file members. There is no audience watching divorce negotiations, and therefore there is no need for symbolic issues.

Another reason appears to relate to the mediator's ability to predict and deal with a reluctance to divorce before a symbolic issue is introduced to sabotage an agreement. Lawyers often relate how an agreement fell apart at the very last moment over a seemingly unimportant item. What this demonstrates is not that the chosen item is significant but that the party raising the issue really never wanted the divorce.

The other model assumption that did not materialize was the expectation that there would be emotional or sentimental items of personal property that would have special significance to one party. This did not arise in any of the cases. Indeed, in all of the cases the couples had agreed on the division of personal property before they entered mediation. Each seemed capable of determining what s/he wanted and the other needed. There were no disputes on this.

The absence of this battle suggests that couples have a sense of fairness about the division of items brought to the marriage by either party. There did not appear to be any particular emotional attachment to property; its division was more a function of practicality.

part III

Case studies

chapter 6

Analysis of nine
mediation experiences[1]

Marvin and Sheila:
A couple who could not divorce

Marvin and Sheila were married in 1960 and have three children, ages fourteen, twelve, and nine. They have been living apart for two years; however, they live in the same town. Both are still closely involved with one another, even though they are also involved in affairs with other people.

They were in joint therapy with another therapist and were referred to me on the basis of a joint agreement to divorce. The therapist briefed me on the key aspects of their relationship, which were borne out by my own experiences with them.

The referral indicated that custody of the children was the main issue and that other items had been essentially settled. In the first session, however, I found that nothing had been agreed to, but that custody was indeed the central presenting issue.

My notes of the first session include the following observation: "The couple is still very angry at each other and fight at every opportunity. It is difficult for them to think about problem solving since their energies are directed at how to use the present experience to continue the attacks on one another. There is a serious question in my mind as to whether they are ready to divorce or whether they need to maintain the liaison—painful as that might be."

My prognosis proved to be very accurate. The couple were basically dishonest with each other and with me. I followed the process outlined in the client handbook, only to find that they resisted preparing any hard data. They came to each session unprepared or having left the material in the car or at home. I asked them to complete the budget data, showing how

---

[1]Certain identifying data have been changed to protect the anonymity of clients.

the money was currently spent. In addition, I wanted to learn more about the exact family income. Marvin was self-employed and his entire income came from fees. He claimed he had had a bad few years and that his income this year was only $8,500. Sheila worked as a receptionist and her income was more easily defined at a regular gross weekly salary of $120. While she was prepared to share her income information with me, she was vague about the expenditures. On the other hand, Marvin was vague both about his income and his expenditures.

They agreed that Marvin gave Sheila no money but paid the basic bills for the house—mortgage, taxes, insurance, and utilities. However, he paid these directly and gave no money to Sheila. She paid for food from her salary.

Marvin used the mediation process as another tool to control his wife. He came to each session with another story to tell me "in confidence" about her and frequently asked me to arbitrate the issues. While refusing to come up with the hard data, he stated on numerous occasions that he would accept whatever I decided—always, of course, carefully controlling the data upon which I would decide the merits. Each time, I rejected his blandishments by reminding him that this was mediation, not arbitration, and that I would not mandate any settlements.

This case demonstrates how clients use one issue as a cover for others. Although the presenting issue appeared to be custody, I did not feel that the husband was serious about his demand for total custody of the children. I felt he was using the custody issue to prevent us from reaching the core of the financial support items. However, I was unable to move him from this, even though I probed hard for some indication of his true feelings.

So I developed a different approach. I asked each of the parties to complete three tasks between sessions:

1. Make an inventory of the reasons the children should be with you. This list should include only the pros—not any reasons why the children should not be with the other party.
2. List what accommodations you are willing to make about the way you will handle the children to make it possible for the other party to agree to your having custody.
3. List what you would need in order to agree to the other's having custody. (This last list was not to be shared with me or each other. I designed it to get each of them thinking about a bottom line on which to build a position.)

This was the only task they both accomplished and brought back with them. Even then they did not complete all parts of the assignment. The results were very revealing. These were the husband's answers:

1. I am more responsible; the children get more structure and organization; therefore, they are more responsible.
2. I have positive attitudes and "can do" values.
3. I am intellectually more aware, read more, and am more socially aware; therefore, the children are more stimulated.
4. I set clear expectations; I am not permissive, so the children know what is expected of them.
5. I have follow-through on these items.
6. I give the children "fun time" and do things with them.
7. I provide the children with a balanced diet.
8. Because of the above, the children are stable—I do not permit infantile behavior.
9. Morality: I would not have women friends over for the night while the chidren are there.
10. I do not use the children as weapons and would not use custody as a weapon against Sheila.

Each of the items was provided through a comparison with his wife and accompanied by a verbal put-down of her. As I explored his commitment to custody, he was very guarded. He said he had not developed either of the other two lists, since he felt that he should have custody because his wife was not fit to have the children; he therefore could not conceive of any conditions under which he would agree to her having custody or his needing to accommodate to her values.

Sheila came in with a very different list.

1. I love the children and they love me.
2. I feed them, clothe and care for them.
3. The children are emotionally secure with me. They speak openly and share their fears with me.
4. I comfort them and they always ask for me when they are ill or upset.
5. I exhibit and encourage feelings and affection, and the children are safe to do that with me.
6. We have an open, honest, and truthful relationship.

She added that it had originally been agreed upon, when they separated two years earlier, that the children would live with her. Sheila also said that she would try to provide the children with some of the discipline Marvin was demanding, although it would be difficult because she was not Marvin.

In reviewing these two lists it became clear to me that the wife's list was focused on the nurturing and love role. With the exception of No. 6, "fun time," the husband's list ignored the nurturing role of the parent. This process enabled me to cut through the rhetoric of the parties to get a clear idea that the custody was a tactical issue being used by the husband. Assigning such tasks is useful in cases where direct discussion does not identify the real nature of the issues between the couple.

Another technique I used in this case enabled the husband to move off the custody issue while not giving it up. After I identified the importance of this issue to each party, I needed to develop a way of moving around it. It seemed clear that custody was a weapon for the husband but a real need for the wife. However, if I simply disarmed Marvin of this issue by confronting his real intentions, I would lose his trust and also leave him without a position in the negotiations. So I first suggested to him that we leave custody until last and then deal with it when all other issues had been settled. He rejected this on the grounds that the support items would have to be negotiated on the basis of a specific custody arrangement and if he did that, based on Sheila's getting custody, and the negotiations broke down, she could go to court claiming he had already agreed to give her custody.

We finally hit upon an arrangement that saved face and his interests. We would leave the custody issue to be decided by the courts and we would negotiate two support agreements, one based on Sheila's having custody and the other on his having custody. I felt this was a safe move, since it indicated his willingness to continue negotiating while at the same time, if I was correct in my assumptions, he could move off the custody issue when the other items were settled.

We never reached that point because after nine hours, when neither would develop the hard data and neither was able to make any movement in the give-and-take discussions around the economics, I recommended that we terminate the sessions until they both were more ready to come to terms. The actual decision to terminate came at the end of a three-hour continuous session. We had reached three different agreements that evening, only to have them fall apart at the last moment. First, Marvin changed his position at the point of an agreement. Then Sheila, who had agreed to a framework that would have led to a financial settlement, said that she could not agree until she called her lawyer. I gave her the phone and the lawyer was not available. And then, once more, Marvin backed out of an agreement just as we were at the point of writing it down. That three-hour session left me exhausted and frustrated. I sat down with both of them and shared my feelings that they did not want to get divorced, they were still emotionally tied to each other, and family counseling was more appropriate than divorce mediation. They seemed more relieved than disappointed at my announcement and returned to their family therapist. I suspect that they will be back for divorce mediation at some point.

My case notes for the final session conclude: "There were some clear warning signals at the beginning that were confirmed in the process. Neither party wanted to deal with hard data. . . .

"On reflection, I could have been more confrontative about specific data developed in the sessions as a means of trying to get some movement. However, this might have made me an adversary of Marvin rather than a mediator for the couple."

Ira and Bev:
A long-term nonmarriage

Ira and Bev have been married for thirty years and have four children, ages twenty-eight, twenty-three, sixteen, and eleven; the younger three live at home. The couple continue to live together, although they have little or no relationship. Bev was in therapy and Ira had just entered therapy. I was briefed on the situation by Bev's therapist.

Ira was a successful accountant until he was convicted of client fraud and served one year in prison. He became involved with another woman about ten years ago.

Bev has never worked outside the home and is still very dependent on Ira, who controls the money. Their total income appeared to be about $13,000 from Ira's salary, plus some money he made on the side selling cosmetics. Thus the economic aspects of separation were narrowly defined.

An event during the first session warned me about the difficulties of this case. After I briefed the couple about my function and the mediation process, Ira said that he was not aware that Bev wanted a divorce. He also said he was not committed to a divorce. I did not deal with this at the time from a belief that this statement might be a ploy on his part. However, had I dealt with this issue in depth at that point, I might have settled the case more quickly.

I identified a need to increase the size of the economic pie as an early strategy. Bev and Ira were barely making ends meet on the current income with one household. I doubted they could divorce or separate on that income. In addition, I felt that Bev could not gain any real independence until she was contributing to the pie. She said that she would like to move to Canada with her eldest son. However, this could not be done unless she were totally independent, since there was no reason to suppose that her husband would provide any support if she moved out of the state.

Both parties completed all of the data sheets, and there were no essential differences between the two budgets. However, in reviewing this section with them I delayed dealing with the future budget for separate households until I had time to explore individually some ideas on how to increase the total income and develop Bev's independence.

In establishing some goals for Bev, I found her to be ambivalent. On the one hand, she wanted revenge—to take Ira for every penny he had to repay her for all the pain and misery he had caused her. On the other hand, she wanted her independence. I focused on how she might get it. She said she had a head for figures and would like to become a bookkeeper. I suggested she consider negotiating an agreement that Ira pay her tuition at a vocational school so she could get a job. I also suggested that she explore with her therapist referral sources for job training and look at the possibility of getting a CETA job.

Bev then said that her job problem was compounded by the inability to drive. She said she would like to learn to drive but did not have the money for it. I suggested she consider negotiating for Ira to pay for her driver's education. She said she doubted that Ira could afford either of these proposals, and I suggested she let Ira worry about that. If he really wanted his independence, he could borrow the money to pay for this.

When I met with Ira to set his goals, I raised these problems in the context of an agreed-upon need for Bev to develop independence. For her to become independent would require increasing the size of the pie which, I suggested, could be achieved either through Bev's working or his taking an additional job.

Ira pointed out that he had already taken a second job with the cosmetic distributorship. He thought the best move was for Bev to take a job. He doubted she could handle school, since she would have few peers at school. He thought she should take a job at a local check-out counter and work her way up; then she could take adult education classses in the evening. He said he would consider paying for Bev to learn to drive if she went to work.

It seemed to me, at the time, that his willingness to finance Bev's driving lessons was based on a belief that she would be neither willing nor able to get the job in the first place.

My notes at the end of the first session discuss the need for them "not to separate now so as to conserve income, while emphasis is placed on Bev's developing independence.

"I am not sure of the emotional consequences of this approach. It appears that it should help ease the transition by focusing both of them on their independent futures. Ira has already made some of the breaks and exercises these freedoms. Bev has not yet moved, and giving her the chance to grow will also enable her to turn away from the marriage more easily. Bev has let her low self-esteem project through her appearance. Giving her power in these negotiations—indeed, making her needs central to the family's relationships during the next period—will be an important step toward restoring her esteem and thus her appearance."

This was all very true. Ira's needs however, continued to interfere with a settlement.

The following week Bev surprised me by announcing that she had talked to her therapist, who had referred her to the local college counseling center. She had gone there and, although "it was full of young people," she was obviously excited and had signed up for the basic bookkeeping course. She was very pleased with herself and a noticeable change took place in her appearance as she progressed at the school.

But as she progressed and grew—her appearance improved, she developed a sparkle and began to enjoy life—Ira's condition deteriorated. He became so depressed that his therapist sent him to a psychiatrist for medication. Ira did not want to break the old relationship. His need for Bev became more demanding, much to the annoyance of Bev, who, in the past, had welcomed it and catered to it.

As this was developing an urgent issue emerged. Ira had asked me to raise the question of the High Holidays with Bev. He wanted to spend them with his sister's family in a traditional way; she did not. Bev did not like Ira's sister, who, she felt, supported all of Ira's weaknesses.

I spent an evening helping them negotiate. Each time I thought I had a settlement, however, Ira sabotaged it. I tried to get them to trade by spending Rosh Hashanah according to the interests of one against spending Yom Kippur according to the wishes of the other. After two hours of negotiating and bickering, I got, according to my case notes, agreement from both of them that the first night of Rosh Hashanah was key, as was Yom Kipper Eve, and then proposed that if all stayed home and celebrated

Rosh Hashanah, Bev would support Ira's taking the children to his sister's for Yom Kippur Eve. Ira accepted this and I urged Bev to do likewise. Bev agreed to the proposal with a nod. Ira demanded to hear her say it, and I intervened, saying that I was satisfied that Bev's nod was as good as her word. I did not want to push her too hard or too far. However, Bev voluntarily stated her agreement. Ira then asked for it in writing. We argued about this for some time and Bev asked me to put it into writing. My draft read:

> It is agreed that the family will spend Rosh Hashanah, September 12, evening together at home, and that the children shall spend Yom Kippur Eve, September 21, with Ira's family. It is further agreed that both parties will support this agreement and encourage the children to follow it in a spirit of family responsibility.

The case notes go on to say, "Ira said 'She'll never agree to that.' Bev said she would agree with it and she would also tell the children that they should go with Ira on Yom Kippur Eve. Again it appeared that a settlement was accomplished. Ira also agreed, adding, 'That means you get Monday and I get Yom Kippur *and* Tuesday.' Bev rejected this new demand."

The agreement fell apart, and we ended the session amidst considerable anger on their part and frustration on mine.

The following week Bev informed me that they had finally discussed the issue during the intervening weekend and had reached an agreement that involved their spending Rosh Hashanah at home for dinner and then going to Ira's brother after dinner, and that Ira's sister would join them there.

I viewed that as a significant victory for them because it was probably the first time in fifteen years that they had been able to reach an agreement about an issue involving their children or Ira's family. On the basis of this I decided not to terminate them—an action I had seriously considered at the end of the previous session.

We then dealt with some of the financial problems. They were in debt for over $1,500, and only the previous week the utility company had disconnected service for failure to pay an overdue bill.

In this discussion I suggested they use the local Debt Counseling Service. (This points up the importance of the mediator's understanding and using the network of community services.) Ira said he would seek a referral from his therapist.

The case was becoming more complicated and it seemed appropriate therefore to analyze it. First I laid out the data as I understood them:

Bev	Ira
Wants him to initiate the divorce so that she could then get Legal Aid to defend the action.	Refuses to initiate the divorce.
Is frustrated over her inability to obtain a divorce—confirmed by the material problems.	Was not sure he wanted the divorce at first session.
Needs to punish Ira. Also wants at least two-thirds of his income in alimony.	Needs her support of his family; wants her to act "normally" toward his family. Example, High Holidays debate.
Wants eventually to move to Canada near eldest son.	
Has taken bookkeeping course as first step toward independence.	Has become despondent with Bev's growing independence.
Needs driver's education to gain greater mobility	Now says he wants a divorce.
Needs dental coverage to get her teeth fixed.	Would like to live in another town near his job.

Goals: First, increase the size of the pie by (1) building up second business venture of Ira and (2) getting Bev employment. Second, help Bev develop confidence to exercise the independence she wants. Third, help Ira focus on the future and the possibility of building his own life following separation.

Strategy: I need to be sure that both are actually ready for the move to separate. I plan to do this by focusing on reality. Ask each of them to list the specific items to be negotiated. Write these down and have each of them sign the list, with the understanding that items cannot be added once the negotiations begin. This will set clear boundaries for their behavior, hopefully preventing a repetition of the High Holidays bargaining. This procedure should also let me know within two sessions whether they are really ready.

The analysis helped me clarify the issues and set limits to my own sense of usefulness in each situation. Out of the analysis came the idea of having each of the parties set a date for actual separation and list what it would be like actually to live apart. (This list was not to be shared with anyone.) I wanted each to understand the reality of separation. For example, I asked Ira to think about what it would be like to come home to a dark, empty room and prepare his own meal at the end of the day. I asked Bev to consider how she would get the clothes to the laundromat without a car or driver. I wanted them to begin to think about the change in life-styles that separation would mean.

This was useful, for they came back with a set date for separation and both talked about what life would be like. I explored with them, at the subsequent session, whether they were actually ready—both economically and emotionally—for a separation, and it was jointly agreed to suspend the negotiations until after the New Year, when Bev had graduated from the bookkeeping course and had found a job. They both seemed comfortable with this approach and, checking back with their individual therapists, confirmed that this was the right approach for them.

When Bev and Ira returned the tension between them had not diminished. Bev had finished the bookkeeping course and was looking for work. However, she had another problem that interfered with that task. Her hearing was impaired and she had never received medical attention for it. She was now in need of a hearing aid to be able to comfortably engage in conversation. She felt that she had missed out on a job because she did not always hear what the interviewer was saying to her.

Ira's response to this new need was to ask if there was some charity that would provide the hearing aid. I pointed out that it was unlikely that the couple could get assistance and that, if he really wanted to move toward a divorce and his independence, they would have to figure out some way of paying for the hearing aid. He said that he thought he and Bev would probably differ over what she really needed and how much it would cost. I called them together and we discussed the problem. Ira said he thought a hearing aid would cost $130. Bev said that it would be at least $800. They engaged in a long and bitter fight about how much it would cost and who was being reasonable. I finally suggested that we do some comparison shopping. They each agreed to check at least two suppliers of hearing aids and to return the following week with quotes. We could then proceed from a basis of fact.

At that same session Ira raised the problem that Bev had called his place of employment to complain about his going out to lunch with a member of the female sales staff. He said it was embarrassing to get these harassing calls at work and that they jeopardized his job.

I spent time with Bev exploring this behavior. She said she had become furious when she realized that he had enough money to take someone out to lunch, while their electricity was cut off because they could not afford to pay the bills. We explored this anger and then looked at some of the business reasons why Ira might have to take someone out to lunch and at whether he or his company paid for it. This individual session gave us an opportunity to again focus Bev on her future goals. She agreed that calling him at work did not help her achieve her independence. I helped her separate her need to hurt Ira for the things he had done to her from her need to build her own life. She agreed to try to work on this aspect so as not to interfere with his work life, which might be self-destructive and prevent her from moving toward independence.

The following week they returned with a series of quotes for hearing aids. The prices ranged from $320 to $1,200. We looked at the various alternatives and agreed that Bev would consult with her doctor as to which was the best, consistent with the couple's ability to pay. Ira agreed that he would pay for a hearing aid by borrowing from a bank, provided Bev stepped up her job hunt. Bev found a job at a local office. The job was part time for the first two months and then full time, paying $9,000 a year. Ira purchased the $360 hearing aid recommended by Bev's doctor.

Consultation with Ira's therapist indicated that Ira was now more ready to proceed with the separation. His despondence in the earlier stages of mediation had been caused by a breakup of his relationship with the other woman at the same time that Bev asserted her need to break with him.

We prepared a new budget. Ira earned about $13,000 a year, and Bev now earned $9,000. The older of the children living at home had moved out to college, and the middle one was holding down an after-school job. Bev decided that she would move out of the rented house to a smaller apartment, if Ira would agree to pay the moving costs, the rental security deposit, and for new curtains for the apartment. In return, she would accept only $25 a week in support of the youngest child.

They negotiated hard over the details of the agreement, finally coming to terms that permitted both of them to live separate lives that could grow in different directions. This mediation was spread over almost six months and required the mediator to move frequently from mediation to therapy. This was another case of premature referral. Both spouses could have handled the divorce more expeditiously had they dealt with all of the emotional issues of uncoupling before entering mediation.

Jean and Jack:
An unmarried couple with a child

Jean and Jack lived together for six years, unmarried. Their son, Joshua, was born in 1973. They separated about nine months before coming to me and have maintained joint responsibility for the son. Josh attends a day-care center, and the parents take turns picking him up and caring for him.

Jean now wants to move to Oregon. They want to mediate the issue of custody. All other items have been agreed upon.

Both parents are loving and clearly feel deeply for the son, and each agrees that the other loves Josh equally. They would really like someone to decree the decision for them.

I asked them to inventory which situation would be best for the son in terms of his interests and accessibility to the other parent. I also asked them to think what each would need in order to be comfortable giving custody to the other.

In these discussions it became clear that in the back of each parent's mind was a concern about the problems posed by the distance between Oregon and New York. Each was asking, "How can I be sure of seeing my son?" even though neither parent specifically articulated this.

I thought that one approach might be to suggest the creation of a Josh Fund, with each parent contributing $10 a week. "This would create an annual fund of $1,040, enough to assure at least one cross-continental trip a year for any one of the three people involved. The surplus could accrue to pay for Josh's education, etc., as he grows up. This would also help clarify the extent to which the possibility of a total cutoff from the child is the major factor in the thinking of either of them."

The following week they returned with their lists. I met first with Jack and he gave me his list:

1. I give Josh lots of love and affection; he looks forward to the weekends. (Jack picks him up from the day-care center on Friday evening and returns him to the center on Monday morning.) We have good times together.
2. The day-care center is a stable place, a good place for Josh to be during the day.
3. Josh has a core of friends at the center and looks forward to going there.
4. The separation from one parent would require less acclimation if Josh stays here.
5. I can provide for him more adequately in general terms and in major areas such as medical.

I discussed the idea of the Josh Fund and he was receptive. He also thought it was a good idea because Jean was always concerned that she contributed less to the family; this way she could make an equal contribution.

Jean and I then met to review her list:

1. Josh will experience a new and more natural environment; he loves to go camping and is happiest when outdoors.
2. He will be sharing these new experiences with me.
3. He will meet new people and make new friends and get an education through travel.
4. We love each other; he needs me.
5. I will be able to spend more time with Josh under my new work/life plans.
6. It will be easier for Jack to come visit us than for me to visit New York because Jack makes more money than I do.

I discussed the idea of the Josh Fund with her and she found it attractive. Having raised the idea with both parents, I was hopeful that the Josh Fund would open the way for some movement in that it built in some guarantees for the absent parent.

We came together as a triad and quickly reached agreement on the principle of the Josh Fund. I then reviewed the two inventories and said that I thought each was valid and that there were no compromises involved in the two lists as they were essentially the same.

So we turned to the second point, accessibility. Each parent presented clear arguments why the other would have accessibility to Josh and Josh to him/her, and in the discussion each could see the merits of the other's case.

I then spent considerable time with Jean exploring the depth of her commitment to go to Oregon. She said that when she and Jack first got together they had spent a lot of time planning to travel and settle in a less industrialized area. However, as they had settled down, Jack kept putting it off and that was a big factor in the decision to separate. She had a whole new sense of living since she decided to make the move. She could stay in New York but at a great cost.

My case notes record, "I then observed that I did not think that a permanent solution could be found at this time. Josh was a lucky guy to have two such loving parents, and since they were not constrained by legal requirements, perhaps we should think about what to do in the next two years and put off a permanent solution until closer to the time that Josh enters regular grade school."

I raised the same idea with Jack. "He agreed to consider the next two years, saying that he had come to the session with a heavy heart; he had no idea how a solution could be reached because there was no room for movement while he had no legal rights. However, he thought a compromise could be worked out for the next two years."

We came back as a triad and I reviewed the individual discussions with both of them. My notes continued, "I pointed out that a two-year plan gave space for experiences upon which to base a permanent agreement. Many changes could take place over the next couple of years. Jean may return to New York. Jack could move West. They would experience living apart from Josh for long periods. Either could marry or live with someone else (Jack had mentioned this as a possibility) and thus change priorities."

I indicated to them that I thought it was time for them to talk directly to each other and that I was willing to suggest some ideas later, if they were unable to reach an agreement.

They both agreed they wanted the Josh Fund. Jack wanted to put more than $10 a week into it, but Jean felt that $10 was all she could reasonably afford in the foreseeable future. They finally agreed upon $10 a week.

Jean then proposed a plan. "Josh would go with Jean for six months, October 1977–March 1978, with a December visit by Jean and Josh to New York for the holidays. Jack would come out West in March 1978 and take Josh for six months, April–September 1978. Then Josh would go back to Oregon for six months and then back to Jack for the final six months. At that time he will be ready to enter first grade and we will decide on a permanent plan during the summer of 1979." Jack agreed to this plan and both decided to open the savings account as of August 15.

The agreement between Jean and Jack was drafted with the minimum of legal language, reflecting their interest in avoiding that approach. It also reflected their "culture" and, given the fact that Jack had tenuous legal rights, did not appear to jeopardize either party's interests.

I gave considerable thought during these negotiations to the advisability of a temporary arrangement that left the son with each of the parents for blocks of time. It could be argued that such shuttling back and forth between the parents would be difficult for Josh to handle. However, I felt that any problems that could arise from this were more than offset by the fact that both parents loved the boy and would provide him with the support he needed.

The plan worked well. Josh went West with his mother; they took about six months making their way across the country. At the end of the period, Jack flew out West and picked up Josh for his stay in New York. At the end of that period, Jean came back to New York and picked Josh up. However, things had not worked out as she had hoped in the West, and she was seriously thinking about returning to New York. The visit to pick up Josh confirmed her feelings, and toward the end of her period of custody she decided to return to New York and chose to reside near Jack, so that they could return to a shared custody arrangement for Josh.

Dan and Cindy:
The two-step agreement

Dan and Cindy were married in 1960. When they came to see me they said they planned to separate shortly, having rented their house and leased separate apartments. They have a daughter, Kriss, aged thirteen, who will live with the mother.

The couple had been seeing separate therapists. They had reached a general agreement on how things should be divided. They wanted to try a long-term separation because they were both undecided about a divorce.

Dan seemed very anxious to establish his fairness and decency. At first this was a factor in the talks. They were both mature and respectful of each other and shared a desire to work out an amicable settlement. The financial terms had already been generally agreed upon and it appeared, on the surface, that theirs would be a simple case. However, developments again showed the importance of the "third ear," so necessary in mediation.

I sensed tension developing as we discussed custody. My notes read, "Cindy was concerned at the fact that Dan had not thought through the specifics of visiting with Kriss. I suggested that they think about the child on two levels. First, we agreed that in talking of custody we defined it to mean the physical location of Kriss; then, we would define each party's responsibility to the child. Cindy seemed comfortable with this and Dan concurred."

During the intervening week they moved into separate apartments. When they arrived back the following week, they were not ready to negotiate. There were real communication and feeling problems that had to be dealt with before talks could resume. The mediator must be prepared to take time out from the negotiations to deal with these feelings. If they are not dealt with they will crop up in some other form, possibly blocking a settlement.

In line with this I spent almost all of the following session dealing with feelings. My case notes explain: "Cindy arrived a little late. Dan reviewed the items he thought they had an agreement on. He appeared tired. He said that Cindy had sent him a letter about custody but had phoned, asking him not to open it. He had it, unopened. He said he thought things were not going to be as easy as they seemed before. 'She's having trouble defining her independence; she wants it but is afraid of it,' he related."

Cindy joined us and Dan gave her the unopened letter. She reread it to herself and said she had been feeling down when she wrote it. I opened the discussion on custody versus responsibility. Dan said he had no problem with it, and Cindy said that the point that concerned her was that nothing was definite about visiting with Kriss. Dan suggested that he pick Kriss up each Friday evening and keep her through Saturday. He said that he had planned to do this the following weekend and that Kriss had agreed, saying she wanted to get back to the mother's home early on Saturday to be with her friends.

Cindy was very uneasy during this conversation. I asked her what troubled her. She said that she did not know how to say it without seeming bitchy. I suggested she had a right to be bitchy, and she ought to bring the concern out into the open.

She then said, with great difficulty—at one point hiding her face in her hands—that she thought Dan did not care about Kriss and would not live up either to the intent or the spirit of the agreement.

Dan responded with emotion for the first time. He said he had suggested a plan of action. He admitted that he did not have a good relationship with his daughter, but argued, "who does with a thirteen-year-old? She wants to talk to you when she's ready. Unfortunately, that's usually late at night." Turning to Cindy he commented, "The thing is you relate or fight with her more of the time. I just don't get into fights with her—you do."

Cindy then expressed her concern over the fact that she found that Kriss needed to be close to her all of the time and that this was putting great pressure on her. She said that Kriss followed her around, was constantly underfoot to the point that Cindy felt she must get out of the house for a while, which, in turn, only made Kriss worse.

I indicated that Kriss's reaction was normal. She probably felt she had lost one parent in the separation and wanted to be sure she would not lose the other. She might also feel that she was, in part, responsible for the separation. The important thing at this point was for both parents to assure her that she was wanted and needed, and that she was not at fault in the separation.

I asked Dan if he had called Kriss since they had separated. He said he had not because the phone was not installed in Cindy's apartment yet. We discussed Kriss's needs and I leaned hard on Dan to agree not only to regular visits for full weekends but also to the importance of his *initiating* contact with Kriss. We finally agreed that as soon as the phone was installed, Cindy would call Dan so that he could make the first call to Kriss.

I then turned the discussion to the holidays. I pointed out that Dan's calendar coincided with Kriss's and that Kriss would often be at home when

Cindy was at work. I suggested we try to develop a schedule that would be beneficial to Cindy and Kriss in terms of Dan's academic calendar.

I made arrangements for Cindy to come in half an hour earlier for the next appointment, because I believed that she had some concerns she was not yet articulating and would need to if the final agreement was to meet her real needs. In the intervening week I drafted an agreement, covering the items they had supplied me with. I had that ready for the next session.

When I shared with Cindy my observation that she seemed uncomfortable about some of the issues, she responded that she thought she was angry and concerned about Dan's feelings toward Kriss. "He really doesn't care for her, and he simply ignores her, and I don't think he will do anything for her or with her once the separation is finalized."

In the ensuing discussion it developed that she believed his relationship with Kriss was one of the reasons for the separation. It became obvious to me that I could not resolve this issue but merely ameliorate the cause. I asked her if she felt that the visitation agreement worked out in the previous session was satisfactory, and she said that if she had it in writing, and knew that Dan was really accessible to Kriss, she would feel much better. I showed her the clause I had drafted and she said that having it signed would make her feel a lot better.

She also discussed the issue of money, saying that she thought Dan had trouble handling money. "Last summer he spent a lot of money on things he really did not need and he is still paying for them now so he's short of money. He asked me to lend him some money, or to take a little less in support, and I don't want to do that."

We discussed this at length and agreed that she should not lend Dan the money or change the dollar agreement, since if these changes took place, the separation would not. Cindy said she really needed total separation from Dan and could not keep having contact with him.

The former point was particularly interesting because Dan had proposed giving Cindy about 60 percent of his net salary—a generous figure compared to the norm. I was concerned that he not agree to this amount simply because he wanted to be a nice guy. If that was the reason, there was a high possibility of his reneging on it in the future when the nice-guy shine wore off.

I spent time with Dan exploring this aspect and was satisfied that he felt the burden of taking care of Kriss justified the support amount and that he was sufficiently comfortable with the proposal to maintain it.

When I brought the two parties together again, we explored the alternatives of regarding support in terms of child support or alimony, and they agreed to consult an accountant to see which way provided the greatest tax advantages. Finally I suggested that Dan and Cindy consider whether there should be a trade-off between the husband's support and the wife's independent income.

The separation agreement contains some interesting items. First there is a provision for maintaining the jointly owned property. This provides some income for the couple and also represents the principle that this is a separation agreement that is not intended, as of now, to become a divorce agreement.

There is also a provision for reducing the husband's support payments in proportion to the independent income of the wife. By defining the support in terms of percentages of the husband's net salary, any increase in the latter also provides a built-in cost-of-living increase for the wife. In this particular case the agreement also recognizes that the husband derives some additional income "off the books," which could not be part of a document of record.

Fifteen months after Dan and Cindy entered into the formal separation agreement, Dan's attorney called me and said that they were ready to convert the separation into a permanent divorce. He indicated that there were differences as to how to divide the property and suggested I reenter the case. I arranged to meet with Dan.

Dan arrived with a clear sense of what he wanted. He told me that he was now living with another woman whom he would eventually marry. He said that he and Cindy agreed that there was no way of putting their marriage back together and that they now wanted to move to a divorce. He did not want to maintain any joint arrangements with Cindy and thought it was best for both of them if they could sort out the property and end all shared relationships. He proposed either selling all of the property and sharing the proceeds or one party taking the summer house and the other the year-round house, with some adjustment for differences in the value. He said he would like to be able to move into the house that Cindy and Kriss now occupied. It was somewhat run-down and he felt he could repair it and improve the maintenance. In addition, since the mortgage rate on the house was 5½ percent, the mortgage payments were very easy to handle. I asked him how he thought Cindy would react to that proposal. He said that Cindy had often talked about moving out of the state and that this might be the opportunity she was looking for. In addition, he said that he knew Cindy and Kriss were having a tough time together, and he would be willing to take custody of Kriss if he could also have the house. He thought he could come up with a down payment of approximately $5,000 to pay to Cindy and then pay off the difference of her share over an agreed-upon period.

We discussed Dan's new life, and he expressed the feeling that he and Cindy had held one another back emotionally during the marriage. He now saw areas that he needed to work on in order to grow. He did not feel that having custody of Kriss would present any special problems—at least no more problems than most fathers have with teenage daughters. His future wife knew Kriss and would welcome her. He wanted to try to keep the summer property because he enjoyed using it during the vacation; he had put a lot of effort into remodeling the house and he was not sure that all his sweat equity could be realized if it was sold now. I indicated that I would explore these various ideas with Cindy and set a meeting date for her.

Cindy's life had not developed in the same constructive way over the past year. She had graduated from college at the time of the separation but had been unable to obtain a job in her field. She was currently doing a menial clerical job, which was unsatisfying and paid little. She had moved back into the jointly owned house because the apartment she and Kriss had rented had not worked out. But upon returning to the old neighborhood she found that the friends and neighbors she and Dan knew related to her differently as a separated woman. Her relationship with Kriss worried her. They often had major fights that ended up by things being thrown at a wall. Kriss pretty much did as she pleased and deliberately interfered with all of Cindy's attempts to establish an independent social life. Cindy related that one evening she had a man friend over for supper. Kriss, who normally would not stay in the same part of the house with her, insisted on spending the evening in the same room, making all three people very uncomfortable.

Cindy felt that Kriss was not spending as much time with her father as she would like, primarily because she would insist on coming home to be with her friends, or simply cancel appointments with the father for the weekend to be able to be with her peers.

Cindy was at loose ends. Her career was not working out, her relationship with Kriss was unsatisfactory, and she had not been able to develop sustained social relationships with other people—partly because of Kriss and partly because of her own frustration with life in general.

I asked her whether she wanted to get back with Dan, and she was adamant that, difficult as her life was, she did not want to return to the marriage. Indeed, she too felt they should convert the separation to a divorce. We explored different ways of dividing the jointly held property.

Cindy wanted to keep the house she was living in and let Dan keep the summer house. I asked her what she thought the difference in value was, and she thought the summer house might be worth $15,000 less than the equity in the other house. She thought that if she could get her career launched, she could pay off Dan either by cash payments from her income or by reducing the support payments he made for Kriss. I then explored with her how she could develop her career. She thought that it might be better if she could move. Or, she said, she had seen a couple of local jobs in her field that looked attractive but they required considerable travel. She could not take these jobs because she was needed at home to take care of Kriss.

As we discussed this Cindy mentioned that she had talked to her therapist about this problem and now realized that she often used Kriss as an excuse for not venturing out into the world. She would like to overcome this fear. I suggested she think about the various alternative ways of dividing the property, and also think about how she could use the divorce to enhance her own future independence.

The following week I met first with Cindy alone. She said she had explored some of the ideas with her therapist, and I then suggested she consider the possibility of Dan having physical custody of Kriss, so that she could launch out and develop her own career. She thought about this and responded that she did not think that would work, because Dan did not have space in his present apartment to keep Kriss permanently. The arrangements were OK for the occasional visit but would not be suitable for a long period. I then suggested we examine alternative arrangements. I suggested that Cindy's future might not be tied to New York but that she may be better off moving to another part of the country where there was a greater demand for people in her profession. I then played out the possibility of Dan having the house and custody of Kriss, while she concentrated on her career. Cindy thought about this for some time and then said that she had thought about such ideas but not seriously and that she needed more time.

We then followed up with a short joint session in which we agreed that Cindy would have the house appraised and Dan would have the summer home appraised. They would bring these figures to the next session, and we could begin to look at the issue with some hard data on hand.

The following week I met with Cindy alone, before Dan arrived, to further explore the idea of changing the custody arrangements. Cindy was torn. On the one hand, she realized that if she was truly single, she could explore a range of career alternatives. On the other hand, she felt that if she kept Kriss, she did not have to take any of the risks involved in establishing a career. However, even if she placed those issues aside, what would people say about her if she gave custody of the daughter to the father? We explored these feelings in depth. Cindy was unsure she could make a move in this area. She was unclear about the best course of action and, anyway, she was not sure that Dan would take custody of Kriss, even if she wanted him to.

I then met with Dan individually and indicated that it was time for him to make his proposal regarding the house and Kriss. I told him that I had not wanted him to put the idea on the table until I was sure that Cindy was ready to hear it. I was now sure that she was ready. We came together for a joint session. I reviewed the work we had accomplished so far, including the two property appraisals. The summer home was appraised at almost $12,000 less than the equity in the other house. We agreed to use that figure as the difference to be negotiated. I then opened the way for Dan to place his proposal on the table.

He proposed to have custody of Kriss and to take both homes. He would give Cindy a cash payment of $6,500 upon settlement, and then send her monthly payments over a period of seven years to pay the remaining balance of the equity in the two houses. In addition, he would pay Cindy 25 percent of his income until she got a better paying job and would continue support on a sliding scale until their earnings were comparable.

Cindy had trouble understanding all of this and we went over it a couple of times. Once the details were clear it became necessary to give Cindy some space in which to consider the emotional implications of the proposal. We suspended negotiations for a month during which time Cindy worked through her feelings; did she really want the freedom that this arrangement provided? Could she live with not being the custody mother?

After some intensive sessions with her therapist, Cindy was able to determine how to proceed. She wanted to take it one step at a time. She moved into an apartment close to her job, and Dan moved back to the house with Kriss. By the end of three months, Cindy found a job with her current employer that required traveling about three months of the year. She visited with Kriss, who, while having trouble accepting her mother's decision, appeared to be developing a less explosive relationship with her father and with Cindy. Cindy was now ready to move to a final settlement. Dan paid her $7,000 plus the remaining equity in the property in monthly payments extending over ten years at 9 percent interest. In addition, Dan paid Cindy 20 percent of his income; this was to be reduced as Cindy's income increased, up to a point where their incomes were relatively equal.

Cindy is doing well in her new job. Her relationship with Kriss is improving, and she has established a good relationship with another man. She is saving most of the money Dan pays her on the equity settlement to build sufficient capital to purchase a house of her own in the future.

Bea and Ben:
Why the children cannot be left out

Bea and Ben have been married for seventeen years. They have two children, a daughter, Alice (age sixteen) and a son, Sam (age fourteen). They live in the same house, although they have had separate living arrangements for the past three years. The decision to separate and divorce was apparently initiated by Bea, who wants to move out of the house.

Ben said that he had already developed most of the budget material but that Bea probably had not. My case notes record, "Bea said that she was in business for herself and had been for a number of years and thought she could get the material together. She indicated that she had been reluctant to move on the divorce until she was sure what she would need and fully understood the details of alimony and child support. Ben said that this was the first time he had heard about alimony, and he thought that the broad outlines of a settlement were already set." The mediator often finds that an issue which has been carefully avoided by the couple is raised in mediation. This occurs when one partner cannot deal directly with the other on the issue. The mediator, however, provides a protection from an immediate emotional or physical response to the idea. Once the couple have discussed the issue openly, it no longer holds the threat to either party. The mediator notes the issue, who raised it, and how, and incorporates that material into the marital power analysis.

The couple apparently had agreed that the son would live with the father and the daughter with the mother, but no details had been developed on how this would work. That the children would fit into the arrangement was taken for granted from the beginning, an idea that was reinforced during the negotiations by information shared with me, indicating that the children related better with the proposed custody parent than with the other parent. As it turned out, this was not necessarily correct and it reinforced my belief that children, particularly teenagers, must be involved in the mediation as arrangements affecting their lives are being made.

This case provided me with some new challenges. First, the wife was perpetually late, often arriving as much as an hour late and once trying to cancel the appointment about thirty minutes after it was supposed to start. I established clear ground rules. The couple paid for the time scheduled, whether they used it or not.

In addition, the wife spent long periods of time on the telephone with me, clarifying goals and questions. I permitted this because I determined that, although she had initiated the divorce, she had little outside support and needed to be able to talk things through. However, it did add considerably to the time spent on the case.

The major areas of disagreement appeared to be over the amount of support, the date Bea would move out of the jointly owned house, and the manner in which the house would be disposed of and the proceeds divided after its sale.

These areas were further complicated by the difficulty of getting any hard data. Ben provided six copies of his W-2 form since all of his income came from salary. Bea, however, was very reluctant to state the specific income derived from her business. Up until the previous year, Ben had managed the books of the business and claimed she netted about $12,000 a year. Bea said business had declined since he stopped handling the books and that she actually only made about $3,000 net this year. The $3,000 figure was slowly increased during the negotiations to "about $5,000." But Ben had secretly opened her bank statements and copied them, showing a gross of approximately $27,500 over the year. He shared these figures with me but did not use them in the actual negotiations.

Unfortunately, the mediator cannot subpoena the records of either party. However, in all the cases in which there is other than salary income, the hard data are impossible to get immediately and slowly change upward as more information is revealed during the negotiations.

Bea and Ben had filed joint income tax returns, but these showed Bea's income at less than $2,000 for tax purposes. No matter how I pressed, I was unable to determine the real income derived from the business, and without that figure on the table, negotiations about the amount of support were very difficult. In order to assist me in my thinking, I assumed that her real income was somewhere between the $5,000 to which she had admitted and the $12,000 Ben had estimated. So I functioned as if it were about $8,000.

I began by dealing with the easiest item of dispute first: the house. Bea had agreed to move out and Ben was to live in it with the son. I then suggested the standard procedure for splitting the equity. However, Ben wanted the right to buy out Bea's share, and she wanted protection in the way in which the value was appraised. She came back with a proposal for each of them to appoint an appraiser, with the two appraisers selecting a third and the actual value to be determined from the average of the three figures. I pointed out that this would be expensive, since appraising was not a charity.

She then came back and suggested that Ben have the house appraised, and that she have the option to buy him out if the price was to her liking. They hassled over this for some time until I suggested that we write into the agreement a clause that I would appoint the appraiser, who would be unknown to either of the parties. They found this acceptable, and we were able to move to another item.

When there is little trust between the parties, they will often suggest complicated and expensive ways of settling an issue. The mediator can save the couple money and build increased confidence in him/her by suggesting more direct and less expensive ways of solving differences.

The issue of financial support was tied up with the true incomes of each party and the date at which the house would actually be sold. Ben wanted to settle for $25-a-week child support. Bea felt she could not live on less than $150 a week. As I tried to move Ben up, he revealed that the price for increasing his payments would be that he could live in the house for as long as he was making child-support payments. His reasoning was that he could not afford to pay child support and live in an apartment.

Alice was almost seventeen; therefore, child support would be required for another year but Ben would be willing to pay until she was twenty-one. On the other hand, I felt that Bea's interests were best served by maximizing support in the immediate future as she found her feet and concentrated on building the business. I therefore went back and forth between them, suggesting $100 a week for child support for a period of two years. Ben would continue to live in the house for those two years, and it would be sold concurrently with the ending of child support. At this point Ben also pressed for establishing a date when Bea would actually move out. He had resolved his earlier reluctance about the separation and now wanted to make the move as quickly as possible. The agreement was reached in a final session that took about three hours. Ben and Bea were very suspicious of each other, which made it difficult for either of them to negotiate directly with the other. At no time did they place any proposal on the table in a joint session. Each new idea or proposal was made to me. I then took it to the other party and described it, taking the answer back to the proposer. I spent most of the time shuttling back and forth between the two parties. I drafted the agreement and sent them each a copy. Ben called to say it was substantially correct, except for a clarification regarding his liability for Alice's college expenses. I suggested he talk to Bea, get her concurrence with the change, and I would then modify the agreement.

Bea did not call. Since we were approaching the Christmas holidays, I did not press her for a response. However, early in January I talked to her, and she said she had some additions to the agreement. She described them to me on the phone, and I identified two as being economic and the rest noneconomic.

I suggested she talk to Ben and ask him if he was ready to reopen talks. I also said that I would be prepared to reopen talks only if both parties would agree on what items were to be added before we reopened the negotiations. She agreed with that, as did Ben, and we set a date for the reopener.

When we met I put the new items in writing and had each party initial the list, agreeing that it was what we would be negotiating about. At this point Ben also added two items. The initial list showed:

1. Revise date for Bea to vacate the house.
2. Make a separate list of the division of property.
3. Provide that if part of the house is rented, each party shares equally in the income.
4. Make the clause "Major Decisions Affecting Alice and Sam" subject to arbitration.
5. Indicate that medical-dental coverage be maintained at present level, regardless of employment.
6. Provide for tuition for Alice after age nineteen, and remove the stipulation that child support will be paid directly to Alice if she is enrolled as a full-time student.
7. Negotiate terms of filing joint tax returns.
8. Incorporate into the agreement the current status of life insurance held by each party.
9. Provide that the children of this marriage shall be the prime beneficiaries of each other's estate. In the event that either parent remarries, the children of this marriage shall remain beneficiaries of not less than 50 percent of the estate.
10. Provide protection of co-signator of the loan.

Item 2 was added because, although both had agreed that there was no problem regarding the division of property, there were disagreements that needed negotiating.

Item 3 was added when Bea learned that Ben intended to rent a room to a friend.

Item 5 was added because the first draft identified the medical-dental insurance as being employer-provided.

Item 6 was added to reflect more accurately what the parties were willing to do for Alice and to provide that the support would continue to go to Bea.

Item 7 proved to be a particularly difficult one. Ben had arranged to be deliberately overdeducted on his income tax. Therefore the couple each year received a refund of approximately $1,500. Bea wanted to guarantee that she shared in one-half of the refund if she agreed to file a joint return.

Item 8 was designed to reduce the cost to both parties of providing life insurance coverage for the children and to recognize the fact that Bea could not carry as much coverage for them as Ben could.

Item 10 was included by Ben. He had co-signed a loan for $5,000 for Bea to expand her business. He wanted an assurance that if she defaulted on the loan, he would not be held responsible for it.

The parties quickly agreed on items 2, 4, 5, 6, 8, 9, and 10, although, in keeping with all other sessions, never directly but always through me. That left three items to be decided. I determined to focus on items 3 and 7 because these had provoked the most emotion from both parties. Ben took the position that if he rented part of the house that was his decision, and since this reduced the attractiveness of the house to him, he felt that he should derive the benefits of the rental income. On the tax item he also argued that Bea's contribution to the taxable income was only $2,000; therefore she should not share equally in the refunds.

Bea argued that the house was jointly owned, and therefore the income belonged to both of them. In addition she questioned now whether she should be the one to move out—why shouldn't he be the one to move? On the tax returns she also felt that if they were filed jointly, the refunds should be shared jointly.

With these two economic items outstanding, I tried to see whether a trade could be made between the parties. I suggested that they share the rental income equally, and share the tax refund in proportion to the amount each paid in. This was done in an exploratory way in private sessions with each of them.

Ben indicated that he might make some movement; I could not get Bea to move on either of the items. At the end of three hours I brought them together and suggested that we were at an impasse that called my usefulness into question. I suggested that Bea think about the pros and cons of the two outstanding economic items. She asked to see me again privately. We caucused again.

In this meeting she expressed her concern as to whether she could make it alone. We explored this concern and the dangers of early remarriage. She said that she had thought about it a great deal and was not ready to get remarried. I then pointed out that she had now been married for almost eighteen years. In two more years she would be covered under Ben's Social Security provisions. I suggested that we explore the idea of his agreeing not to convert any separation agreement until the twenty-year date had passed.[2] This seemed to ease some concern for the future. However, she was still unable to compromise on any of the outstanding items.

---

[2] This provision was recently reduced by Congress to ten years.

I met with Ben and explored the idea of limiting his right to convert the agreement, and he concurred, so I added that to my list of items.

We then met again as a triad, and I said that I thought we should have one more session with a strict time limit. I said I was willing to meet once more for no more than two hours—starting from the scheduled hour. If we had not reached an agreement within that time, I would terminate the process and recommend that they each retain an attorney and fight it out.

At that point Ben asked me what I thought was fair. He said he would like to know what I would recommend. I said I normally did not reveal my ideas since that placed me more in the role of an arbitrator. However, Bea also asked me to suggest what I thought was fair.

I then told them that since the house was jointly owned, I had sympathy with Bea's position that the income should be shared. On the other hand, I did not sympathize with her position on the tax returns. I said that I thought each party should share in that portion of the returns for which they contributed to the taxable income.

Ben said that he thought that was fair, and he could live with it. Bea smiled and said that she thought it was fair, and she could live with it. They both looked at one another, surprised that they had reached an agreement. I then introduced the last item, the date Bea would vacate the house. She said that she would need at least until June—six months—to vacate. Ben said he thought she should move out by January 31. I said I thought that a slightly later date would be more appropriate and suggested February 28, aware that any deadline would be difficult for Bea to meet.

I drafted the revised settlement. The second round of negotiations reinforced two beliefs I had held: the advisability of having the final agreement reviewed by an attorney, since a review by a third party allows for identification of special items that may have been overlooked, and the advantage of intervention in order to assist the parties to (1) set goals, (2) identify areas of disagreement, and (3) identify solutions to those areas. This case helped me to understand the importance of intervention at the appropriate time to assist the parties in reaching an agreement instead of making the agreement for them.

About a week after I had mailed the revised agreements to the parties, I got a call from Bea. She said she did not know whether she could sign the agreement because Alice had announced that she wanted to stay with her father through the end of this school year. If Alice stayed with the father, Bea would not get the child support, and without that $100 a week she did not think she could survive alone.

Bea related that Alice had told her she did not want to leave her school right now, and that Alice had suggested that Bea come up to the house a couple of times a week to cook for her, because Alice and Bea ate health foods, while Ben and Sam ate junk food.

I spent a long time on the telephone with Bea, trying to help her identify whether the reluctance to make the move was hers or Alice's. I pointed out that it was only natural for Alice to be reluctant to change schools in mid-year. However, Alice had to understand the consequences of the separation and be prepared to accept her share of the dislocations.

On the other hand, if it was Bea who really did not want to go through with the move, she needed to think through what to do. At this point, Ben seemed reconciled to the separation and if Bea wanted to change her mind, some form of counseling would have to take place to redefine their relationship. Bea ended the phone consultation with the thought that she had to deal with Alice so as to be able to make the move.

A few days later Bea arranged for a session for herself and Alice with me. I also suggested that Ben and Sam meet with me and added that I wanted to meet with Alice and Sam alone. The time was set. I began with Bea and Alice. At this meeting, Alice made her case that she did not want to move because of her friends. We talked about the need for the separation and Bea's relationship with Alice. I helped Bea establish the fact that she was indeed going to move out and go through with the separation and ended the session with the comment that if Alice wanted to stay with the father, I would simply help them all to renegotiate the financial arrangements to permit Bea to leave and Alice to stay.

I then met privately with Alice and explored her feelings regarding each of the parents. She clearly did not relate well to the father and wanted to stay with the mother. However, she did not want to leave her school friends at that moment and thought that if she could delay the separation, she might also prevent the divorce. I tried to clarify for Alice the fact that (1) Bea was moving out and that I would help negotiate a different arrangement to make that possible for Bea, and (2) there was nothing she could do to stop the divorce, just as there had been nothing she had done to cause the divorce. I then suggested that she think about different plans, such as being able to spend weekends at the house so that she could visit her friends after she and Bea had moved.

My discussion with Ben and Sam convinced me that the living arrangement for them was what both wanted. It also appeared that Sam would be just as happy to have his sister move out, so that he would be the only child.

I then met again with Bea and Alice. After a lot of tears and assurances that arrangements could be made for Alice to return to the house for visits whenever she wanted, and after assuring Alice that Bea really intended to move out, Alice agreed to go with her mother. All five of us came together for one final session to clarify for each party exactly what would happen. Ben agreed that Alice could come up for weekends whenever she wanted. I then went around the group explaining what each would be doing, their rights and responsibilities. Bea and Ben signed the agreement the following week, and the household divided within the agreed-upon time. In six months Alice spent one weekend with her father and brother.

This case demonstrates the importance of involving the children in the decisions that affect them. Such an involvement limits the fantasizing about the possibility of the children reconciling the parents. It also limits the children's sense of responsibility for the end of the marriage. Finally, it gives the children an opportunity to make their own needs part of the final agreement, thus making it easier for them to live with the inevitable parental decision.

Milton and Jane:
The husband who did not want rules

Milton and Jane were married in 1966. They have two sons, Dean, born in 1971, and Donald, born in 1973. Shortly after the birth of the youngest son, Milt found another woman. At first he refused to have any relations with Jane. "I didn't think it was fair to be doing it with two women." Then Jane learned of the relationship and they moved into separate rooms. Milt finally moved out of the house in January 1977, and they have been living apart since then.

They have an open visitation arrangement and he visits the house frequently. A number of times they dined together before coming to mediation.

Milt currently gives Jane $800 a month, and she earns $240 (net) at a local nursery school. Milt spent a lot of time assuring me that he really loved the kids and cared for Jane. We discussed what each thought might be the major issues. Jane thought it might be a specific piece of furniture, since they had agreement on support and custody. Milt said he thought the house would be a major issue. He wanted to sell it and split the equity, which he could then use to set up house with the other woman.

We agreed that since they had separate budgets in operation, there was no need to use the information in the mediation material. Instead, we established dates for each of them to spend time with me in developing goals.

I asked Jane to share her goals for the next couple of years. She said, "To live through each day." She said she still had a lot of feelings toward Milt to work through. We explored whether she could increase her independent income, but this did not seem possible because of the children's needs for her time. In addition, Milt was very insistent that she be a "good mother" and devote all of the time to the boys.

She said she had not contemplated marrying again, and I asked how the current visitation arrangements affected her social life. She said that Milt honored her requests not to come on specific days and to leave early when asked. She then went on to describe her relationships with other men, and I sensed her need to validate her attractiveness despite Milt's rejection. This occurred in the sessions and sometimes afterwards. On one occasion we left the office together and she wanted to stop, chatting socially, and dropped a glove on the floor, which I let her pick up herself. I recognized her need for this kind of validation but only intended to provide it within the bounds of my mediation role!

We talked about what she wanted in the agreement, and she said she would like to have Milt take the children out on Sundays rather than stay with them at the house. She would also like to have a clear understanding on how long he would keep them, so that she would know how long she had to herself on those days.

The money arrangements seemed adequate. She had gone through her expenses for the past six months and found that she was just living within her income.

A meeting with Milt followed and we explored his goals. Milt said he did not get along too well with his father, so he felt that it was important to him to have a good relationship with his sons. He complained that the boys were often unruly, and he had to do a lot of disciplining when he went over to the house and did not like that.

I asked Milt if their relationship was different when he and the boys went out together. He said he had not been able to take the boys to his furnished apartment, because it was small and "crummy," but that he hoped the settlement would enable him to move to a better place.

Milt had another suggestion regarding the house. He said that Jane's mother had money. Could Jane borrow $5,000 from her mother to give to him to set up his new place? He would then sign over $5,000 of the equity in the house to her.

I suggested that he not raise this as an idea with Jane. I assumed she would explode if he did, but at the same time it gave me an idea of a source of cash for Jane to buy out Milt's equity and thus gain another measure of independence, if it did not affect her relationship with her mother.

Milt said he would maintain the current payments, and he wanted the same visitation rights. He did want an agreement that the boys would always keep his family name, and that they would always stay in New York. He did not want any of the furnishings, claiming that he did not want to take anything away from the children.

The situation following individual sessions revealed the following goals:

Jane	Milt
House: an important security to her and the children.	Need for decent apartment with livable furnishings.
Will stay in current job, which gives maximum opportunity for nurturing the children.	Willing to maintain support amount—wants adequate mothering for children
Milt to take the children away from the house all day on Sunday and to return them at the prearranged time or pay the babysitter.	Same open visitation rights. Boys always to carry his name.
To share in any increase Milt receives in his income.	Jane and the boys always to live in New York.

Developing lists in this way helps identify areas of common agreement and possible trade-off items. Reviewing the latter with the parties together helps establish the mediator's credibility and assures him/her that they hear the same thing at the same time.

I decided to open the joint discussions on the issue of visitation. Milt's frequent claim of a special love for his children indicated that this should be one of the easier items. He was very reluctant to agree to any specific arrangements. He said he did not like to be told what to do and that he would have trouble thinking of things to do every Sunday. I suggested he read *Creative Divorce* (Krantzler, 1974) for some ideas on how to relate to his children in this situation. He finally agreed to take them out of the house but not necessarily each Sunday. He then agreed to each Sunday, after Jane assured him that she would not insist on it if something came up on a specific date.

I then moved to the idea of Milt's taking the children for weekends. Here he was even more resistant. He said if Jane wanted a weekend off, she should ask her friends to care for the children. He said he did not mind having the children, but that he wanted to decide when. Slowly he moved toward agreeing to take them every other month for one weekend. He then backed off, asking what would happen if he wanted to go out that Saturday night. I suggested he could plan ahead for those six nights a year, and he finally agreed to six weekends a year.

Of the cases discussed here, three of them involved a struggle by the wife to get the husband to take a greater role in relation to the children. The assumption in dealing with custody and visitation is that the children will be used as tools against the husband. In the three cases mentioned, the opposite was true: the husbands wanted total freedom from their parental responsibilities and had to be forced into a greater role.

I met with Milt after this joint session and suggested that he think about what his best interest was in connection with Jane. He said he thought her interest would be served best if she remarried. I asked him not to think about it in terms of Jane's best interest but of his own. I pointed out that if she remarried it would reduce his financial obligation to only the boys, and enable him to develop a better relationship with his girl friend. I then pointed out that increasing Jane's chance of developing her own new social life depended on her being able to find arrangements for the boys. Thus, taking the children for a weekend would increase Jane's opportunities for developing a new social life and, therefore, remarriage, which was in *his* best interest.

Once both parties really understand and gain a measure of comfort with the idea of legitimate self-interest, the negotiations move more smoothly.

Another important aspect of mediation appeared during this visitation discussion. At one point Jane was very angry and frustrated and said, "Forget it Milt, I don't need it, just forget the whole thing."

I refused to let the matter drop because I knew that in their normal relationship, Milt would have won his point simply by reducing Jane to frustration and getting her to drop the matter. Certain patterns of behavior that exist between the parties will, of course, be part of the relationship during the negotiations. Where those patterns interfere with open and equal negotiations, the mediator must intervene to circumvent the normal behavior and permit the negotiations to continue.

Often one side will have the preponderance of power, only because the other side believes that imbalance to exist. In those cases I spend time with the client who does not recognize her/his own power in the relationship to identify that power and help her/him to use it in the negotiations.

Thus there are many ways for the mediator to intervene in the negotiations to facilitate a settlement. But these interventions can become interferences unless the mediator understands that the reason for the intervention is to assist the negotiators to reach a fair settlement.

My next meeting with these clients was also marked by a learning experience for me. I met with Jane and she was unhappy with the outcome of the visitation negotiations. She said this was in part because Milt had revealed his true feelings toward the two boys. He really did not want them. But she was also afraid that we had pushed him too hard and that if she pushed him she would lose everything. She said that Milt only did things that were his ideas. "If he thinks he is being told to do anything, I'm afraid he will just walk away and stop all payments."

She then said that she thought she might be better off with an attorney, because she felt that through the court she would probably get about $600 a month, and the certainty of that $600 was better than the constant fear of losing all $800.

This question was a probe of how effective I was going to be compared to an attorney. Most clients raise this issue at some point in the mediation process.

Understanding this enabled me to deal with my own inner panic at being questioned, and instead of switching the subject immediately to safer ground, I was able to use the question to increase my effectiveness.

I asked Jane why she thought a court awarding her $600 would be better than her own agreement for $800, when her own agreement would also have the force of law. We talked about the difficulty of enforcing court-ordered agreements. She then revealed that she was not sure how far to push or go and was not sure how to use me to help get what she wanted. We spent a long time talking about this, discussing what I could do and developing ways for Jane to use me. She felt much more comfortable after this discussion and seemed to be in greater command of the talks from then on.

She was also testing me to see just how much of an advocate or supporter I was going to be for her. This also required that I make it very clear to her that I related to Milt in a similar way, helping him identify his strengths and ways of using me.

At least once in every case one or the other party asks me how I keep from taking sides. Couples are always wondering what goes on in the private session with the other. I deal with this by being as supportive as possible during the private sessions, helping the client to identify his/her own specific self-interests and developing the best way to present those interests. While we are engaged in this cooperative project—essentially the two of us versus the one sitting outside—I am always careful to point out that I follow the same process when meeting with the other party.

I try to help the client understand that this impartiality is necessary to increase the negotiating efficiency of both parties and to assure the best possible final settlement from everyone's point of view.

After these two sessions the nature of the negotiations changed. Jane was more assertive. She took a firm stand against borrowing money to buy out Milt's share of the house equity. She was also firm on the amount of the support. She was willing to give Milt some of the furniture, but Milt said that he did not want any of it.

In the final session it was Milt who made the major concessions. He gave up on the idea of selling the house and agreed to write in the $800-a-month support.

This became a major victory for Jane because she not only achieved maintenance of the status quo, which she wanted, but also removed Milt's power to unilaterally alter the conditions of the separation.

It was also a victory for Milt because it meant that he was a step closer to making choices about his life. He could now begin to cut the cords to his first marriage, which he had not been able to do very successfully thus far.

He could also plan more clearly for the future and therefore develop a better relationship with his girl friend. But probably most important of all, the settlement was the first step toward taking responsibility for his own actions.

Eileen and Tim:
The dishonest couple

Eileen and Tim were married in 1971. They have one child, Leah, age five. The husband moved out to live with another woman in the fall of 1976 and failed to provide any support for Eileen and Leah. Eileen went to Family Court for "support proceedings" and won a court-ordered wage garnishment of $50 alimony and $25 child support each week. Along with the $114 a month Eileen receives from SSI for Leah, who is handicapped, this is just enough to keep them off welfare.

Eileen had applied for and received welfare before the Family Court action. However, she was reluctant to apply again, because the Department of Social Services had applied a lien against the equity in the house. This meant that, should she sell the house at some future date, the DSS would reimburse itself for its support of her from the proceeds of the sale. The lien already totaled $3,000, and she did not want to increase it.

She moved out of the house and now rents it for $300 a month, although the monthly bank payments are $311. Tim recently signed over the house to Eileen. He is in debt and signed over the house to prevent his debts being used as a lien against the house.

Eileen's goals are (1) for Tim to maintain the current financial arrangements, even if she gets a job; (2) to provide life insurance protection and keep any interest in Tim's pension plan for Leah; and (3) to control Tim's visitation rights—she particularly does not want him to take Leah to the house of the woman he is living with.

We discussed the pros and cons of going through with a divorce rather than settling on a separation with the court-ordered (and guaranteed via garnishment) weekly payments. Eileen said that she would like the freedom of the divorce, provided she could include the court order in the settlement agreement.

Tim's goals are to maintain the current open visitation arrangement, to divide the house equity when the house is sold, and to reduce the amount of support payments. He earns about $17,000 a year, with a take-home check of about $245 a week. Therefore the support payments represent about 30 percent of his net.

When I brought them together to review the two goal lists jointly we started with visitation. Eileen had two points. On the one hand, she wanted a regular schedule of visits. Apparently, Tim's visits had been sporadic and rarely more than once every other month. On the other hand, she wanted to control where he took Leah when he had a visitation day. In the past he had spent the day with Leah at the wife's apartment and Eileen did not want that in the future. She wanted the freedom his visitations should provide her.

Again, this part of the process required my intervention. I first defined the husband's role and moved him toward agreeing to visit Leah more often. I then helped Eileen to see that there was no way she could know or control where Tim took Leah on visiting days.

Part of this was accomplished in the joint session and part in private sessions. During the latter, I became concerned that neither party seemed committed to living up to the agreement. They both indicated that they would agree to specific points only because they had no intention to keep that part of the agreement.

I reviewed my notes following the sessions and realized the importance of their remarks. It is not always possible to identify trends or signals at the time they appear because, despite the distance, mediators still become involved in the dynamics of the immediate situation. Therefore, case note reviews often help identify important aspects of the case. I then take note of them and check them out at the next session.

At the beginning of the joint session I asked the couple if there were any joint debts. Both shook their heads negatively, and we passed on to other items. At one point in the talks a credit card was mentioned, and I probed further on the debt issue. It then turned out that there were joint debts with Bank Americard, a bank loan, and balances with five department stores. These debts came to over $1,500 and it was clear that neither of them wanted to talk about the debts. It is important for the mediator to watch for any apparent deviations from the normal profile and to probe those deviations to be sure that they are real.

For example, in every case I have handled so far, debts have been larger than normal and a cause of friction between the parties. Therefore, part of the profile of an average divorcing couple will probably be sizable debts. Absence of debts would be unusual and should not be accepted on face value.

As I moved back and forth between the parties during this session, I found that each of them made concessions too easily. I tried to prevent premature concessions but each made them. Tim and Eileen basically reached an agreement that evening, and I agreed to draft it for them. I was uneasy in this because of a number of points. For example, Tim did not want to file a joint tax return with Eileen. Since all of his income came from salary, it was clearly in his best interest to file a joint return and pay less tax. However, since he apparently had little intention of living up to the agreement, he apparently did not want to have to share any information with his wife.

I decided to schedule another session just to deal with this honesty question. It seemed to me that neither of the parties understood the consequences of entering into an agreement that they did not intend to keep. It also became clear to me that this couple saw me as a cheap lawyer and not a mediator. They merely wanted the document and the divorce, with a minimum of give on their part and a minimum of expenditure.

This is another danger the mediator must watch for. The couple must have some commitment to the idea of mediation and at least a minimum of respect for one another to be able to negotiate. If the mediator picks up signals that neither of these two basics are present, s/he should terminate the clients and advise them to use the traditional legal route.

During the intervening period Eileen called me on the phone and said she wanted to cancel the whole agreement. I replied that this was okay with me, and that I was available should they want to reenter talks. I also advised her to call her husband and inform him of her decision.

She then said that what she really wanted was for me to call Tim and tell him she was threatening to cancel the agreement, because she thought he was demanding too much, and see what he said. I explained that I could not do that. My role was that of a mediator, and if she wanted to cancel or test Tim she would have to deal with him directly.

I again advised her to get in touch with Tim and to get back to me should they decide to resume negotiations. Neither Tim nor Eileen called back.

Mark and Ethel:
The martyr wife

Mark and Ethel have been married for twenty-seven years. They have four children, aged twenty-one, nineteen, seventeen, and fifteen. The eldest is married, the other three live at home. They were referred by a social worker at Catholic Charities. Mark is a New York City policeman; the family lives in suburbia. Ethel had assumed that when he stayed over in the city, he slept at the precinct house.

The children gave Mark and Ethel the money for a weekend marriage encounter for their twenty-fifth wedding anniversary. While at this encounter session Mark broke down and told Ethel that he was living with another woman during the week.

This arrangement became institutionalized over the next two years since Mark was unable to make a definitive move, and Ethel was unable to change her martyr role. Ethel had received advice from priests, nuns, and her therapist to break the pattern. On weekends she did Mark's laundry, dyed his hair, and got him all set for another week in the city.

Based on the information I had received from the referring therapist (who was working with Ethel; Mark was not in therapy), I decided to begin by meeting with each of them separately to see where each of them stood. In effect, this first session became a counseling session for each of the parties, but it was important in setting the stage for the separating negotiations to begin.

Mark has risen in the ranks to a responsible position. He is now studying for a degree, and he met the other woman in this program. He is confused in his desire to move out. He still feels drawn to his family and is obviously strongly influenced by his religion. On the other hand, he is drawn to the new woman by her education, his growth potential with her, and the more interesting life he sees as a possibility.

His relationship with Ethel seems to follow the Divorce Adjustment Process model of one party pushing the other to initiate the divorce. He has constantly pushed Ethel to the point of breaking so that she will, in effect, kick him out. Thus the burden for his actions falls on her.

Mark is concerned about all the hurt he is causing people; he is very sorrowful about the pain he has given his family and wants some signal that it is okay to move out of the marriage.

I helped him think about how to set goals for himself that could be realistically achieved in the negotiations. He left with the goal-planning material and the understanding that I would conduct a similar session with Ethel.

Ethel is a martyr. She has been a volunteer in the church all of her life. She has not developed intellectually in the same way as Mark. However, she has lots of innate intelligence and can carry her end of the conversation. She did not finish high school and has tried three times, unsuccessfully, to complete the equivalency diploma.

She behaves like a mother to Mark and also totally mothers her children. She enjoys being wanted and doing for others, although at times she is completely overwhelmed by the consequences of this role. She has great trouble setting goals.

When I first asked about her goals, she said she would like to see Mark live alone in the city for a period to show him what it was like. We explored whether this was realistic, and she agreed that Mark would not give up the other woman. So I returned to what it was *she* wanted.

Ethel said she would just like to pack a couple of bags and move out on her own for a while and let Mark deal with all the problems. As we talked about this she revealed her frustrations with the children. She is also a martyr with them. She related a story of how, after she had dug a path from the backdoor through a five-foot snow drift, her fifteen-year-old son, who had given her no help, told her she was dumb and that she should do that kind of work rather than try to pass her high school tests.

The children are angry at the tension in the family and the parental separation and want to maintain the façade of a normal family by having their father come home each weekend. They express their anger at the mother, particularly now that she is beginning to say that she does not want Mark home each weekend.

Ethel could not think about any goals since she still had to talk about the raw deal she had experienced over the years. We achieved some movement after I explained that she had now been advised to terminate the current arrangement by two priests, a nun, her therapist, and a close friend. She said that even though she was deeply religious, she could see it was time to do it. She could not see a divorce but thought a separation, which defined each of their rights and responsibilities, would be good.

We also talked about her need to start doing things for herself rather than always giving to others in an essentially unresponsive setting. I suggested she print a card to look at a few times each day that says, "God wants Ethel to do things for herself."

She needs some confidence that she can develop a life of her own after the end of her marriage. Mark has a new direction in which to go. Ethel, as of now, does not. My main goal in these negotiations was going to be to help Ethel identify what she really wants out of life and to translate those desires into concrete, negotiable goals.

For example, we spent some time talking about the weekend visits. I asked her to think about some alternatives to Mark's spending the weekend at home. Could he take the children to the city? Need he sleep over at Ethel's on Saturday night when he visits? Does she have to be home when he visits? How can she develop maximum flexibility?

I gave her the material to look over, and we agreed to hold the first joint session after she had an opportunity to review the material.

In the next two sessions with Ethel and Mark, I helped Mark understand the stress he was causing the family by his refusal to act on his decision to move out to live with the other woman during the week. I helped Ethel think about how she could become more independent. And for the first time they did this together.

Ethel handles the money. Mark sends his pay check to her, she cashes it and gives him money as he needs it. She then runs the house and the finances. While on the surface this makes her more independent, in fact it maintains her dependence on Mark. She needs to arrange the finances so there is always money when he needs it. She is dependent on him to be taken care of. For as long as she is deeply involved in taking care of him, she can never find time to take care of herself, with all of the risks that that involves.

I suggested that one weekend she either arrange for Mark to take the children completely out of the house instead of coming home for the visit or leave the house herself for the weekend and take a trip, leaving Mark to take care of the details of running the house. This would give both some idea of what separation means. They agreed. Mark stayed in the house all weekend, and Ethel took off to Atlantic City for a long weekend. It helped her understand the value of independence and while away, she apparently discussed her marriage problems with the friend who went with her.

When she returned Ethel could shape demands to make on Mark for the first time. She wanted to limit the number of weekends he could come to the house. She thought that he should only come one weekend a month, and she would take off for that weekend. If he wanted to see the children at other times, they would have to go to the city to be with their father. She wanted an agreement that provided that she would get Mark's checks, could deduct a specific amount from them, and pay the rest to Mark. That way she would know exactly what she would get and would not have to worry about Mark having enough money to see him through the week.

They agreed to have the house appraised and to establish the current equity with an agreement that when the house was sold, Mark would receive his current share of the equity. A concession to Mark provided that the house would be sold when the youngest child reached age eighteen. All of the other issues fell into place.

But before we could enter into the agreement I called the whole family together for a family conference. The three children still at home came with the parents. I structured the time as a conference, essentially telling the children the facts of the current arrangement between their parents and spelling out the terms of the separation agreement. I told them that while neither parent was willing, for religious reasons, to actually try to divorce, it would be important for them to understand that it was unlikely that the parents would reconcile their differences and get back together. To reinforce this point I mentioned that the house would be sold when the youngest child reached age eighteen.

The children were not particularly comfortable in this session and it was clear that they were not used to discussing family business with both parents present. I sought to engage them in a discussion of the agreement, without much success. I then suggested that the parents leave us for a while, and, without Mark and Ethel there, the children began to open up.

They each realized that the marriage had been dead for a number of years. They were angry about the father but afraid to express their anger to him. Because there had been no family life for as long as any of them could remember, each had developed an independent life with tenuous links to the family.

All three children approved of the settlement and expressed the hope that perhaps now their mother would not spend so much time weeping. I asked if any of them would like to change any aspect of the agreement, and they all replied that they would like to be able to visit their father in the city. When I met again with Mark and Ethel, I related this discussion to them and urged Mark to try to structure his life so that his children could either individually or collectively visit with him some weekends.

I drafted the agreement. Ethel checked it, first with her priest and then with an attorney. Mark chose not to use an attorney, relying instead on the advice Ethel received from hers. They subsequently filed the separation agreement and are now living with it, each building independent lives.

Ellen and Brian:
The powerless husband

Ellen and Brian were married in 1971. They have one son, Bill, born in 1975. Ellen initiated the divorce when, following family therapy, she realized that her growth depended on her independence. Brian opposed the separation and agreed to it reluctantly. He moved out the day before the first mediation session.

Their financial situation is difficult. Brian earns $10,000. The rent on their apartment is $150 plus $50 for utilities. In addition, the renter must work ten hours a week for the owner. Brian has moved into a room costing $90 a month.

Brian paid the rent for the month and also gave Ellen food money. She is looking for a job and hopes to have an independent income. They agreed that she should not get alimony and wanted me to help establish the amount for child support.

They would have liked me to mandate this, but I explained my role. I then helped them ask the appropriate questions to determine what *could* be paid and then measure this against what *should* be paid.

Brian answered all of the intake questions, including Ellen's address. He appeared to dominate the relationship, although Ellen struggled against the domination. However, as the sessions proceeded it turned out that this was a role Ellen played for me. Later she exerted herself, and it was she who dominated the relationship.

Brian feels hemmed in by his job and low pay and is concerned that the costs of separation will further reduce his chances for growth. He has a very good relationship with Bill, who came to the first session with them. Bill was relaxed with both parents but seemed, during this time, to relate more to the father. Brian did almost all of the caring of Bill and this appeared natural.

Brian left the car with Ellen; his $90-a-month room is within walking distance of his job. Both say they have agreed to the property division, with most items staying with Ellen and her agreeing to keep Brian's things in storage.

At the second session Ellen announced that she had been asked to leave the apartment because she could not do the work required as part of the rent. She was now looking for another apartment, and she wanted Brian to pay the deposit and the cost of moving. He did not want to do that. She also said that she had a good chance of getting a CETA job, which would give her some independence.

In his individual session I spent some time with Brian trying to get him to think about what he wanted out of the separation. He said he had given Ellen the car and had been substantially supporting her for the past month and was now faced with the prospect of having to help her relocate. This added to his depression, because it meant that he had less chance than ever to develop his own interests. It also meant that he could not take a different job if that involved a reduction in his income. He said he felt more hemmed in than ever while Ellen, who called him an old stay-at-home, was doing all the things she wanted to do.

We talked about this situation and looked at things that Brian would like to do. He said he was interested in the cinema and politics. I suggested he join the local community cinema club, which could bring him into contact with people of similar interests.

A discussion with the referring therapist at this point indicated that Ellen's parents had interfered with the marriage and were capable and willing to support her move away from Brian, and that this should be kept in mind.

At the third session we had narrowed the issues. Ellen had been hired at about $9,200 a year. So the issues now were how much child support, how to divide the income tax refund, and how to finance Ellen's relocation.

I remembered the earlier discussion with the therapist and suggested to Ellen that she consider asking her parents for help with the move, since it was obvious that Brian would have a hard time coming up with the money. She agreed to think about that.

I then turned to the question of child support. I pointed out that Ellen would have to spend some of her income for child care, and that the cost of child care could be reduced by Brian's caring for Bill part of the time. Brian works nights and is able to care for Bill during some of the days. After some give and take, they agreed that Brian would care for Bill two days a week and Ellen would arrange for child care for the other three days.

That left us with the issue of how much child support. Brian had joined the cinema club in the intervening week and appeared to have enjoyed himself there. Now he was more careful about how much he paid. I took them through some mathematical exercises. I added the two incomes together (hers including child support) and then divided this figure by two. This left Brian with a larger share of income, so I suggested that they look at that figure. Ellen appeared to approve of an arrangement whereby Brian would give her 10 percent of his income in child support, and he seemed willing to pay. This left Ellen with more than Brian in recognition of her custody of Bill.

However, before we could move on, Brian wanted some assurance that the child support figure could be stated as a percentage of income as well as an absolute amount, because he had a chance of getting a job in his field as a teacher where the starting pay would be about $1,300 a year less than his current janitor's pay. They agreed to that as a principle.

We then decided that if Ellen's pay exceeded Brian's by more than 15 percent, his payments would be reduced to only 5 percent of his salary to reflect his low income. I suggested that if Brian's pay was at the Bureau of Labor Statistics' median income, he should not pay less than 10 percent regardless of Ellen's income; they agreed to that proposal, and the formula was developed based on these understandings.

We then had only one item open: the income tax refund. Ellen said that they owed her parents some money for the car. Brian said he had given Ellen a lot more money than they had agreed to before they separated, because she had not gotten another job as quickly as they thought. After some give and take they agreed to use the refund first to repay Ellen's parents (that allowed the parents in turn to help her with the relocation). Ellen then agreed that Brian should keep whatever was left to replace the additional money he had given her.

This was another case where the first order of business was to increase the size of the pie to be divided. The problems of maintaining two separate households on less than $18,000 are going to be considerable; on $10,000 it would have been virtually impossible.

The other issue here involved the husband's having less power than the wife and being originally maneuvered into paying her more than he could manage, which in turn made him even more helpless. He was helped to break out of the pattern of helplessness in part by the additional income generated by Ellen and in part by sharing the automobile, which he needed because of his own involvement in new groups, such as the community cinema.

Finally, in line with my philosophy regarding custody and access, the couple developed a sharing arrangement for the custody of Bill that also helped alleviate their money problems. Brian paid for his child support in part by his caring for the child two days a week. In the process he also maintained a good relationship with his son.

part IV

Conclusion

chapter 7

Some implications for practice

Balance versus neutrality

When reading the case studies presented in the previous chapter, the reader will probably ask how the mediator retains neutrality. Obviously s/he does not. The mediator is not neutral, rather s/he maintains a careful balance between the couple. At times the mediator leans on one party to move from an unreasonable position; at times s/he suggests strategies to the other party that increase that party's power in relation to the spouse. Doing this calls for balance rather than neutrality. How, then, is balance maintained?

In a broad sense balance is achieved by adhering to the broad principle that the mediator is not committed to either party but to the final agreement. In implementing this principle it is useful to establish a set of guidelines against which to measure one's practice. Once the guidelines have been established in terms of the outcome of the divorce mediation, the mediator can measure the progress of mediation against these guidelines and determine whether s/he has succeeded by checking the final agreement. If all of the guidelines have been substantially met, the mediator can be satisfied that balance has been maintained and divorce mediation has been successful.

I have drawn the following guidelines from my own experience; I believe, they direct my practice during mediation and measure it upon completion. A successful divorce mediation can be said to have taken place when:

1. there has been full disclosure of all the economic assets of the marriage,
2. the economic division of the assets and the necessary support payments are essentially equitable and designed to meet the joint needs of the family and the individual needs of each member,
3. there are no victims as a result of the agreement,

4. the channels of commmunication between the ex-spouses are open and direct; the mediator will have helped the couple organize a direct way to make decisions about the children,

5. the couple relate to their children as parents, not as spouses, through the acceptance of the permanence of their parental roles in the context of the ending of their spouse roles,

6. the children are able to develop and maintain an ongoing relationship with both parents; thus the agreement must provide for direct communication with both parents along with an appropriate range of access options regarding both parents,

7. the couple are empowered to make decisions and given the skills during mediation to continue the decision-making process in their respective futures,

8. the extended families, particularly blood relatives, are protected in their relationships with the children, and the children enjoy the same open access to them as to their parents.

Economic issues

The first two items on this list are the easiest to measure. The budgeting material in the client handbook helps to develop all of the assets material (see Appendix A). Often one party will only be vaguely aware of the extent of these assets or may simply overlook them. For example, few wives recognize that they have a shared interest in the husband's pension plan. While married, the couple deferred some income in order to build a pension for the time "they" would retire. Since they will no longer retire together, they will not share this asset. Thus some thought should be given to how to provide the wife with compensation for the loss of her interest in the husband's pension plan. This can be done in part by guaranteeing her an irrevocable interest in the early death benefits which are part of most pension plans. Each solution, however, must fit the specific needs of the couple.

It is my experience that the self-selection process by which people choose divorce mediation over the traditional adversarial method is reflected in the openness most couples display toward one another regarding the marriage assets. However, when that is not so, and you feel there are hidden assets in the marriage and this belief is shared by the other spouse, you will need to develop strategies with that spouse to unearth the information. An excellent guide for doing this is Aspaklaria and Geltner's *Everything You Want to Know About Your Husband's Money . . . and Need to Know Before the Divorce* (1979). Since this advice is combative and assumes that the couple are adversaries, it should not be given to the wife without some careful preparation on how to use it within the mediation framework. The book appears to cover all issues likely to emerge in a contested divorce and has specific strategies for obtaining all the information needed.

The equity of the final economic agreement is determined by a general sense of fairness as to what each party should give and receive from a settlement, consistent with what is available. Identifying how much is available is easier than deciding how to distribute it among the parties. As I point out in the client handbook (Appendix A) both parents will have to determine at what level they want to maintain their children. If travel, horse riding, ballet school, and other benefits of a middle-class life-style have been available to the children, and if money is available to continue this practice after the divorce, the amount of child support will have to cover such expenses. What is more likely is that since two households will now have to be maintained with the income that previously maintained one, there will be a reduction in the standard of living for all parties involved, including the children. The mediator makes sure that the reduction is equitably shared by all members of the family.

Victimization

This leads us to item three: there must be no victims of the agreement. Since the spouses are the prime architects of the agreement, they will usually be able to protect their broad interests. When this does not happen, the mediator can intervene to create situations where self-interest is identified and legitimated. The Ellen-Brian case (p. 120ff) is a good example of this—I helped Brian become involved in the community group and thus have a need for the car and fairer share of the income.

At times the interests of the children and of other family members are overlooked. When this happens the mediator presents her/himself as the guardian of the interests of the other parties, injecting their interests into the negotiations. The mediator informs the couple when s/he is doing this and assumes the role of spokesperson for the absent family members.

The mediator must act forcibly to protect the interests of an absent family member if the actions of the spouses tend to victimize that person. The victimization is identified and the couple confronted with the consequences of their actions. In most situations the couple will modify their positions and mitigate or undo the victimization. If the action only mitigates the circumstances, the mediator continues to press the couple for further modification, until the danger of victimization is removed. What happens if the couple will not rectify the problem? Then the mediator has an ethical responsibility to remove her/himself from the negotiations. A mediator cannot help draft a separation agreement that results in the victimization of a member of the family.

A case example

Sue and Bill came to divorce mediation with most of the issues already agreed upon. Or so they said. They had been married for four years and had a seven-month-old daughter. Sue was very close to her family of origin, to the extent that she was unable to develop an appropriate marriage relationship with Bill. Bill's ties with his family were loose. His behavior, particularly concerning the use of money, was modeled on his father. Bill spent money freely and seemed unconcerned about handling significant debt. Sue, however, was concerned. Her family had always saved for a rainy day and proudly claimed to have always lived within their income. This conflict about money spread to other areas of the relationship and after three months of family therapy, Sue became adamantly committed to a divorce. In the process she convinced herself and Bill that he was the cause of their marriage breakup. They were unable to use therapy to move beyond the money issue.

The referring therapist warned me of the hostility between Sue and Bill, and it quickly became apparent that Sue's hostility was a critical part of her conviction that she was blameless in the divorce. Her only fault was to have married Bill and then, having married him, not to insist that he take better care of the finances. Since she was "innocent" and Bill was "guilty," the proposal they made involved Bill's taking responsibility for all of the debts as well as making a small child-support payment. Sue planned to move back with her parents; her mother would care for the child while she went out to work to support herself, independent from Bill. Because of this independence, and because Bill was the "guilty" party, they had agreed that he would not have any visitation rights.

They presented this proposal at the first session. I reviewed it with them, pointing out that the daughter, Dawn, would be victimized by this proposal. The cost to her was the total loss of her father. Did they really want to do that to Dawn? Sue said she was clear about it and Bill concurred. Of course, Bill's reward for accepting the "guilt" was a minimal child-support payment of $15 a week. I felt there was also a tacit agreement between them that he would not have to maintain payments for too long and, provided he continued to accept total responsibility for the divorce and pay the price of not seeing his daughter, he would also not have to worry about Sue enforcing the child-support provision once he ceased making payments.

I once more spelled out the consequences this agreement would have Dawn. Again the couple indicated their willingness to accept these consequences. I then confronted them and told them that if they, as parents, did not look out for Dawn's interests, I would act for her. I pointed out that I would not continue as mediator if they insisted on denying Dawn her rights of access to her father. Sue protested, saying I had told them that it was their agreement and that I would help them negotiate it. She charged that I was now changing the rules by refusing to help them negotiate an agreement on their terms. I responded that I was willing to help them develop their own agreement but only in the context of their being mindful of the best interests of Dawn. Sue asked me to leave the room for a while; she wanted to talk privately to Bill.

They asked me back about ten minutes later. Sue said they had thought about what I had said and were willing to modify their proposal to take Dawn's interests into account. They would like the agreement to say that when Dawn was two years old Sue would review the situation and, if Bill had changed his ways and become a good influence on the daughter, Sue would allow some visitations. I was unwilling to accept the new proposal on two grounds. First, it meant they would still be negotiating two years from now, and my experience indicated that items left open for further negotiation led to more disputes later. Second, and more important, the proposal still victimized Dawn. All children have the right to see their fathers and to develop a relationship with their fathers as they grow. The modification still denied this basic right to Dawn and therefore victimized her.

Sue was very angry with me as well as with Bill. I told the couple that I was unwilling to continue to mediate their separation if they were unwilling to accept Dawn's rights in this matter and suggested that if they wanted to victimize their daughter, they would have to find someone else to implement that kind of agreement. I wanted to discuss with them a different form of marriage counseling, since it seemed to me that they had not yet resolved the marriage issues and therefore could not properly resolve the divorce issues. But they would not hear of any further marriage counseling.

Bill and Sue probably went to see attorneys and got their divorce on the terms they wanted—both abdicating their responsibilities as parents as they fought as ex-spouses.

Statement of nonconcurrence

In this case I maintained my integrity by refusing to be a party to an agreement that victimized Dawn. The mediator does not simply facilitate a divorce; s/he does it within a value context. Not all cases are as clear-cut as that of Bill and Sue. O. J. Coogler points out that there are times when the agreement may not be in one spouse's best interest but does not specifically victimize that spouse. In those instances he recommends a statement of nonconcurrence (1978, p. 26–27). Coogler notes that "Even though [the mediator's] nonconcurrency does not invalidate any agreement reached by the parties, it can have a significant impact on whether the court will approve the settlement" (p. 26).

The problem with relying on the court to act as the final arbiter is that, with the increasing number of divorces passing through the courts, it is unlikely that an uncontested divorce will be closely reviewed by the court. One study indicated that the court hearing for uncontested divorces took an average of four minutes (Mnookin & Kornhauser, 1979, p. 956). In some jurisdictions an uncontested divorce can be accomplished through the mail, simply by filing the appropriate forms. It is unlikely that the courts scrutinize the contents of such divorce agreements very closely. In those jurisdictions where the uncontested divorce is reviewed by a judge in open court, a statement of nonconcurrence can protect the mediator's ethical responsibility to the parties without invalidating her/his role in the entire situation.

Opening communication channels

The fourth measurement of a successful mediation is the development of open and direct channels of communication between the ex-spouses. If this is to be achieved and maintained, the mediator will want to help the couple limit the range and number of issues dependent on subsequent communication. Although it is easier to put off some decision making in the divorce process, I try to avoid leaving items open for subsequent negotiation. By the same token, the mediator also helps the couple understand the danger of agreeing to something now with the idea of renegotiating later. That is why, in the early stages of the mediation process, I try to deal only with principles, translating them into specifics only when the principles have been firmly established.

The mediator works to have the couple deal directly with one another. In the early stages of mediation the communication pattern is dominated by the mediator. S/he is in command of the process and also acts as the switchboard for the participants. The couple direct most of their comments and questions to or through the mediator. In the early stages the mediator accepts this function, waiting for the couple to become comfortable with the process before moving to direct conversation. Most couples are not encouraged to speak directly to one another until both spouses have a clear sense of their goals. Once the mediator is sure that mutual goal clarity exists, s/he begins to suggest a slight shift in chair and body positions, so that the couple face each other and talk directly to each other. As they deal directly with each other in the negotiating sessions, direct and open lines of communication are being established for them to use after the divorce.

These direct lines of communication are developed in other ways as part of the divorce mediation process. For example, one partner will often speak for the other, describing his or her feelings as well as actions. When this happens the mediator should intervene in the traditional pattern of communication and help establish the need for each partner to speak for him/herself. I do this by first identifying the behavior to the couple. I reinforce the understanding by identifying each subsequent example of speaking for the other. Then I develop a signal I use to the person when s/he is speaking for the other. I intervene each and every time the behavior repeats itself, until the party self-corrects and leaves the other to speak for her/himself. At the same time I work with the person being spoken for to enable her/him to speak for her/himself and with the couple to accept the legitimacy of self-expression.

Including the children

The fifth goal of mediation is to have the couple relate to the children as parents and to accept the permanence of their parental roles. That requires that the agreement recognize the rights and responsibilities of both parents and the right of both parents of access to the children. The mediator knows this has been achieved when the parents accept the various clauses on the joint responsibility of the parents to the children (see Appendix B, p. 175). At times this might require changing the existing relationship between the parents and the children. In Chapter 3, I described the case of Gary and Ruby. The alliance between Ruby and the younger daughter threatened to further weaken an already tenuous father–daughter relationship. In strengthening the father–daughter relationship through the negotiating strategies, I also helped redefine the mother–daughter relationship from a sister–sister alliance to a more satisfactory parent–child relationship.

In moving toward goal number six, the mediator is helping to restructure traditional family relationships. This is done partly by involving the children in the negotiations in a way which is probably unique in the life of most families. The children come to the bargaining table as partners—not necessarily as full partners but nevertheless as partners. The mediator makes sure that they understand the reason for the divorce, the permanence of the decision, and the neutrality of their role in the decision of their parents to divorce. Freed of the fears caused by ignorance of what is happening in the talks, the lack of control over their own lives, and the imagined responsibility for the divorce, the children can focus on negotiating an arrangement with both parents that is in their mutual interest. Thus the more options available to the family for future relationships, the more likely they are to work out a unique arrangement that assures access of both parents to all the children.

Empowerment

Goal number seven calls for the empowerment of the couple. I believe that empowerment is at the heart of all professional intervention. Intervention that does not empower the clients to take charge of their own lives, to make their own decisions, and to understand enough about the past to be able to avoid replicating the undesirable aspects of it, is, in my opinion, unacceptable intervention. In all mediations one or both parties ask the mediator, "What do you think?" Or, finding themselves unable to resolve an issue, they turn to the mediator in exasperation and plead, "You tell us what to do, and that will settle it." These requests are seductive. The mediator knows from a range of experiences what might work with a particular couple. S/he has a good idea of what the outcome of this particular dispute should be. However, each blandishment to tell the client what to do must be met with a reframing of the issue, to help the couple look at the problem from a different perspective in the hope that they can find their own unique solution to each specific disagreement. As they do this, the couple are empowered as a couple to solve their differences. They are also empowered individually to use those skills in other aspects of their lives.

The extended family

Finally, the mediator has goal number eight in mind as the agreement is being formulated. The extended family is often overlooked in divorce proceedings. The grandparents have the right of access to their grandchildren. The children have the same right of access to their grandparents in the future as they have enjoyed in the past. The mediator listens and notes how the family currently relates to the parents' families of origin to be sure that any significant changes caused by the separation are understood. If the changes are too great, the agreement should be modified to protect the extended family's interests.

The mediator's function

When the couple have completed the agreement, the mediator reviews it against the eight guidelines. If any of the guidelines are not being substantially met, s/he tries to identify the reasons and checks to see whether further discussions would remedy the situation. In doing this the mediator should be clear about what values s/he brings to the mediation.

The mediator must always remember his/her primary function, that is, to facilitate the negotiations of some other persons' divorce or separation agreement. When the agreement is drawn up it belongs to the couple and affects their future lives and the lives of the children. Therefore the agreement should reflect their needs.

For example, in Chapter 3, I suggested options that are available to the couple, which, in my view, ameliorate the impact of the divorce on the children and open the possibility of a good relationship between both parents and their children, regardless of which parent has custody. These options are not always attractive to all people. Many couples will be more comfortable with the traditional custody, controlled-visitation arrangement. That is the norm, an arrangement they can understand, and one that is familiar to most of their family and friends. If they therefore choose this traditional arrangement, it is the mediator's responsibility to facilitate an agreement that meets that choice.

The mediator has the power to influence the couple in any given direction. However, if s/he moves the couple too far out of an acceptable pattern, the possibility develops that although the arrangement is written into the agreement, the couple actually operate under their own idea of what is proper. In that case the mediator has helped draft an agreement that will be honored in the breach, with all of the consequent legal dangers.

Although the mediator has the responsibility to honor the choices of the clients, this must always be tempered by the mediator's values. We have seen from the guidelines that a mediator must work from a baseline of values. When the values of the mediator and those of either or both of the couple clash too sharply, the mediator has a responsibility to discuss this with the couple. The guidelines provide a measurement of the consonance of the client's and the mediator's value systems. Within these broad parameters the mediator must decide when the value systems are so different that there is no longer a shared commitment to the outcomes embodied in any one of the guidelines. If these differences cannot be compromised, either the couple will quit or the mediator should terminate them. The Sue and Bill case was a clear example of this, as was the situation with Tim and Eileen. The guidelines are used by the mediator to check on the progress and the outcome of mediation; they are also used to sustain his/her value system.

Mediating temporary separations

When working with couples the therapist is often faced with the possibility that a trial or temporary separation would help the couple examine the marriage from a new perspective. However, suggesting a temporary separation demands that the couple also be able to reach an agreement on the terms of the separation. If the wife is staying in the house, she needs to be sure of continued financial support. Otherwise, the uncertainties associated with the lack of such assurance will prevent the most useful emotional aspect of the separation.

The husband in this case may feel that a temporary separation exposes him to charges of abandonment, which could undermine his case should the couple ultimately wind up in court contesting the divorce. The material in this book can and should be used by therapists to facilitate the arrangement of a separation so as to make the most therapeutically productive use of the separation period. The terms and form of a temporary separation agreement are basically the same as for a separation agreement that is specifically designed to lead to a divorce. Although not every item has to be detailed with the finality of a divorce agreement, as much as possible should be included for the protection of both spouses. With all of the practical, economic, and physical issues secured in a temporary separation agreement, the therapist can help the couple focus on the emotional issues with a greater likelihood of resolving them, because the separation tensions will not be exacerbated by unnecessary disputes over money and the like.

Using a second opinion

A number of clients were referred to me by other therapists because they had reached a dead end with the couple, not necessarily because the latter wanted to divorce. There seems to be a danger for divorce mediation to be viewed by some family or marriage counselors as an appropriate place for their "failures." That is, if the couple cannot resolve the problems with that therapist's help, there is no hope for the marriage. With this type of referral the mediator has a number of ways to determine whether mediation is appropriate and whether the couple does indeed want to divorce. But what of the situations in which the therapist becomes the divorce mediator? Obviously, some of the readiness indicators used by the mediator are valid; furthermore, a clearly inappropriate move to divorce will not be implemented by a reluctant couple. However, the power of the therapist in relation to the couple is greater than the power of the mediator in relation to a newly referred couple. The therapist-mediator might be able to persuade the couple to do things that are not necessarily in their best interest.

This raises the ethical consideration of a factor that can be applied to all forms of therapy and working with people: the use of the second opinion. In cases where a therapist has been working with a couple and they all arrive at a mutual agreement that divorce is in the couple's best interest, it is incumbent upon the therapist to obtain a second opinion before proceeding to divorce mediation. The original perceptions can be checked and the decision to divorce either clarified, supported, or reversed by another expert who has no investment in the specific outcome. Therapist-mediators should develop a referral relationship with other therapists in the area who can provide a second opinion before the final decision to divorce is made.

Moving between mediation and therapy

The mediator may move from mediation to therapy in specific situations. Usually this does not alter the relationship the mediator has with the clients. The goal—to facilitate the separation agreement—is clear, and the mediator works to help achieve that goal. However, there are times when the mediator may want to help the couple clarify whether they do indeed want to divorce, or the need arises for the couple to understand more clearly why they are getting divorced. In the latter case, if the lack of understanding about what went wrong in the marriage is blocking a smooth movement toward a separation agreement, I will share my concerns with the couple and suggest time out to look at what those blocking issue are. Time out involves a separate agreement with the couple. The mediator identifies the blocking issues and suggests that the couple might want to look at them without necessarily having to problem-solve them. If the couple agree that knowing more about the whys of the marriage will help them achieve their goal of divorce, the mediator negotiates with the couple to establish the amount of time to be spent doing this and the goals of such time spent. When this agreement has been reached, the trio can focus on those blocking issues within the broader context of negotiating the separation agreement. Once the blocking issues have surfaced and been dealt with, the couple can return to the task at hand and complete negotiating a separation agreement.

An example of time out

Pete and Pam had been married for twelve years. The marriage had been stormy for the last four years and, following a few marriage-therapy sessions, the wife declared that therapy did not work and asked for a divorce. When the couple arrived at my office the husband was verbally reconciled to the divorce but had not accepted its reality. After a beginning discussion it was clear that he did not believe the divorce would work, because "there's not enough money for us to live apart."

When, despite their joint income of $30,000 a year, he held to this point of view, I suggested time out to look at the marriage. The wife balked because she believed that this was another attempt to put the marriage back together again—something she did not want to do. The husband thought it was a good idea. I spent time clarifying the actual purpose of time out; it was not marriage counseling, it was not to discuss whether the marriage could be "saved"; rather, it was to see how each could better understand the reasons why they were now talking about divorce. I pointed out that if they did not know and share what it was they did not get out of the marriage, they would probably also have trouble knowing what they wanted to get out of divorce. As the terms of the time-out device were clarified and specified, both spouses accepted the idea, and we scheduled three sessions. The first was to look at the husband's perspective, the second at the wife's, and the third to draw some implications from those two sessions.

At the first session I asked the wife to be patient with me, explaining that I would probably spend most of the time talking to Pete. I turned to Pete and asked him, "Pete, what was it that, as a man, you did not get out of your relationship with Pam?" Pete could not identify anything. I reframed the question in a dozen different ways; Pete could think of nothing seriously wrong with the marriage or his relationship with Pam. "Oh, perhaps I got angry sometimes when she didn't keep the house tidy, but it was nothing serious." I worked hard at getting Pete to identify the deficiencies in their relationship because as long as he saw nothing seriously wrong with the marriage, there was no reason for him to divorce.

I modified my plans for the second session. Instead of directing it primarily at Pam, I decided to use Pam's version to provoke Pete's feelings. I opened the session by asking Pam for her ideas as to what she, as a woman, had hoped to get out of the marriage and did not get. Pam articulated her feelings of being taken for granted, not respected, and missing compassion from Pete. Rather than pursue these items with Pam, I turned to Pete and asked him what he thought about each one. Slowly I engaged him in talking about those items, first, by allowing him to defend himself and then by turning him toward his own feelings about each item. Finally he began to agree that the marriage had not been exactly what he had hoped for either.

From this exchange I was able to get the parties to look more closely at the expectations each had brought to the marriage and the fact that those expectations had not been met. In the third session we were able to list the key areas in which the couple differed in the marriage. Pam liked lots of physical closeness; Pete preferred not to cuddle or be involved in "that teenage stuff." Pete wanted a mother for his children; Pam wanted a partnership that included her going out to work to earn extra income for the family. Finally, the major difference emerged; Pam had had an abortion which Pete had opposed.

As they listed these differences they began to see that there had been little chance for success of the marriage from the beginning. Neither was to blame for the ending of the marriage. They were both nice people with different expectations. This session also helped Pete see that he was not really happy in the marriage, and that he could not be happy in the future with Pam unless he or she was prepared to change drastically. Pam was already working, and Pete could not agree that this was right for his family.

When we ended the time-out sessions, Pete understood the end of his marriage more clearly and was able to move toward formalizing it with an agreement that protected his interests as father of their two children. The money issue diminished and, while they did suffer a drop in their standard of living, divorce was possible on their total income.

The time out in this case was specific and focused. Pete and Pam were clear about it and understood the therapeutic point of the sessions. It strengthened their understanding and helped them focus on their future rather than hang on to an unresolved past. The mediation was facilitated by removing major roadblocks that could not have been negotiated away, and the integrity of the mediator was maintained because the couple knew when I was acting as mediator and when as therapist.

Training for mediation

Some therapists feel that the details of mediation are difficult to integrate into practice. It demands a knowledge of law, budgeting, and negotiations. A natural concern arises over the need to be sure that all aspects of a separation agreement have been covered. One way to deal with this is to purchase a Do-It-Yourself Divorce Kit from a reputable source. These kits, which are designed for the layperson, will guide the beginning mediator through all of the issues needing attention. The material in the kit, along with the process outlined in this book, can be integrated into the individual therapist's practice.

Those wanting a more structured approach to mediation should consult O. J. Coogler's *Structured Mediation in Divorce Settlement* (Lexington Books, 1978). Subtitled *A Handbook for Marital Mediators*, the book explains a different method of mediation which is carefully structured step by step. It includes all forms used by Coogler and provides background information on the Family Mediation Association. In addition, the text lists the essential areas to be covered in any separation agreement. The therapeutic perspective is based on transactional analysis.

To complete your understanding of the legal aspects of divorce, identify an attorney in your area with whom you could work. Look for an attorney with a humanist approach. Lawyers specializing in matrimonial affairs will not usually be receptive. The bulk of attorneys prefer not to have to deal with matrimonial cases; they dislike being caught in the emotional storm that swirls around divorce. Lawyers who do not specialize in matrimonial matters usually take divorce cases with great reluctance and would appreciate learning of alternatives. They may even enjoy working with a mental health professional.

Although the Bar Association Canon of Ethics is vague about joint practice, some partnerships are being developed as lawyers and therapists offer joint service to couples "where both the legal and therapeutic aspects of divorce can be explored and clarified" (Black & Joffe, 1978 p. 2). This approach can be expanded where sympathetic lawyers can be found.

Training for mediation is available from three sources. The author conducts mediation training, the Family Mediation Service conducts workshops for mediators, and the American Arbitration Association also offers training for mediators.

The workshops conducted by the author cover the full range of skills required by a mediator from understanding the emotional context in which the divorce takes place to applying the theories of mediation and functioning in the role of mediator. The author also conducts short-term workshops for agencies and continuing education programs around the country. A ninety-minute color videotape demonstrating the author's method of mediation is available for rental along with a training guide.

The Family Mediation Service was formed by O. J. Coogler to develop professional standards in this new field and to provide training for mediators. The training follows the model outlined in Coogler's book and is offered as a 100-hour package spread over ten weekends.

In 1978 the American Arbitration Association announced the formation of a Family Disputes Section. The AAA has a long history of arbitration and mediation in labor management disuputes and in settling disputes in the textile, building, and garment industries. The AAA offers conciliators, mediators, referees, and arbitrators to families in dispute. This is a new direction for the Arbitration Association, and in setting up this service, the organizers reached out to mental health professionals for mediators.

However, the program is designed to use family lawyers and the fact that the AAA is dominated by the legal profession may limit achievement of a full role within the Association by other professionals. The training offered by the AAA is a direct application of labor mediation principles to marriage and family disputes. It is limited by its lack of emphasis on the emotional issues. However, the training received at the AAA entitles the participant to serve on the panel of mediators for the Family Disputes Services of the American Arbitration Association.

Addresses for Further Information Regarding Training

John M. Haynes, Ph.D. School of Social Welfare Health Sciences Center L2093 SUNY Stony Brook, NY 11790	Training information and videotape rental
Family Mediation Association Training Division 2959 Piedmont Rd., N.E. Atlanta, GA 30305	Training and membership infor- mation
American Arbitration Associa- tion Family Disputes Services 140 W. 51st Street New York, NY 10020	Addresses of regional offices

Practicing in an agency

Where can divorce mediation be practiced? This book presents the case for expanding clinical practice through the addition of mediation skills. However, many therapists may not have a large enough number of divorcing clients to warrant adding this skill to their private practice. It should be noted, though, that there are other areas in which to practice mediation, ranging from the local family court to the local family service agency.

Many family agencies are concerned that despite the best efforts of their counselors, couples still decide to divorce. At present, when a couple make that decision, the family agency ceases to serve the family. However, a number of agencies are adding divorce mediation to the services they offer. When this service is offered by an agency, it is usually run by one person, unless the caseload warrants an expansion. The mediator works with the other therapists, receiving referrals from them and consulting with them if necessary.

Agency practice has many advantages. There is a built-in caseload and referral system. If a couple have had a good experience with a therapist at the agency, they are likely to trust the referral to mediation. In addition, the referring therapist is always available for consultation about difficult aspects of the couple's behavior. It is helpful for the mediator to be able to check out perceptions with another mental health professional who has worked with the couple.

The mediator working in an agency also has a range of services to use during mediation. In the Ira and Bea case, I used the other services offered by the Family Service Association where I practice to make referrals for job training for the wife, for credit counseling for the couple, and for welfare advice regarding the hearing aid. A simple phone call linked me with a colleague who picked up that aspect of the case, making my mediation role more effective. "Networking," that is, knowing where to refer to and where to get things done, is an important part of any helping professional's work. In mediation it is essential because most couples have a multiplicity of problems that can affect the mediation process. No one person can solve all the problems, but knowing where to send the clients to get the problems resolved means that the mediator can concentrate on her/his function and not be impeded by either having to try to deal with these extra issues or having them prevent successful mediation. Thus, even when mediation is practiced privately, the mediator should develop a network of referral sources for the problems divorcing clients are likely to bring. The most important of these are debt counseling or debt relief, social casework services, and adult education services.

Working in prepaid legal plans

Prepaid legal services constitute another arena for divorce mediation. Many unions are negotiating for prepaid legal plans paid for by the employer or are establishing their own services using union funds. Many of the problems union members bring to these plans are family problems and often not legal ones. Two approaches here may develop a relationship between lawyers and mental health professionals, while providing new services to working-class people. The first would be to approach union officials and lawyers responsible for the prepaid legal plan to discuss ways in which the mental health professional can assist the service in dealing with nonlegal family problems. This could provide the basis for the development of mediation services at the legal clinic. The mental health professional could advise on referrals for nonlegal assistance and work with the plan, doing preliminary intake for subsequent action. Here the therapist would help the lawyer to identify the specific nonlegal problems that affect the family and recommend appropriate action. Since many of these problems deal with family disfunctioning and potentially with a divorcing family, divorce mediation as a service flows logically from this work.

The second approach would have the mediator contact the officials of the prepaid legal plan with a straightforward proposal for the addition of divorce mediation to the service. The argument can be made on two levels. One, that the use of divorce mediation lowers the family turbulence during the divorce, making "different" behavior less likely on the part of the union member. This is important to the union official who handles the many industrial discipline problems that lead to suspensions or firings when the worker exhibits behavior at the work place in reaction to events going on at home. The union benefits by a lowering of the number of grievances it has to handle. Two, and this is purely financial, divorce mediation costs considerably less than the adversarial legal process. The average mediator's fee is $40 per hour, with average mediation consisting of twelve hours. Thus, a completed agreement can be reached at a joint cost of $480. Add to that the normal legal fee of $250 for an uncontested divorce, and the average union member can obtain a divorce using this method for less than $1,750 compared with the $3,000 or $4,000 a couple spend on a contested divorce. Most unions are eager to offer services that save their members money and services are generally made available through a union's Community Service Committee. It is usually a Community Services Director who acts as the liaison with the professional world in regard to service delivery. Initial contact with a union should be made through the Community Services Director.

Working in the courts

Divorce is a major problem for the courts. Many court systems are overbooked, trying to hear more cases than they can reasonably handle. Waits of nine to ten months are common for no-fault divorces and contested divorces often have to wait for a year or more to be scheduled on the court calendar (Mnookin & Kornhauser, 1979, p. 956). Although it is unlikely that the courts will assign original divorce cases to mediators, because each client is already represented by an attorney, it does appear that the courts are willing to have child custody problems handled by non-lawyers as one way of finding a solution for unresolved issues before the case goes to trial. More research needs to be done on this matter. In thirteen states the courts have established conciliation units as part of the divorce process. Mental health professionals in the conciliation units spend most of their time on problems involving children. Mediation is being used in some of these situations to help find legal solutions to custody questions in a humane way. The mental health professional mediates the custody–visitation differences that could not be resolved through the attorneys; the result is then taken to the judge for incorporation into the final finding.

Conciliation seems particularly appropriate in instances when the couple return to court to complain that the original agreement has not been honored or that circumstances have changed. When a couple continue to fight over the children, it is often the result of unresolved issues from a marriage that was held together through the children. So while it is unlikely that the courts will allow non-lawyers to handle the economic aspects of divorce, it appears increasingly likely that the courts will turn to the helping professions for assistance in resolving custody and visitation aspects of a divorce agreement.

The Association of Family Conciliation Courts, made up of judges, lawyers, and mental health professionals, is very interested in mediation as a method of conflict resolution. You can check whether your state has a conciliation court and learn more about the association by writing to:

Larry Hyde, Executive Director
Association of Family Conciliation Courts
Nova University Law Center
3100 S.W. Ninth Avenue
Fort Lauderdale, FL 33315

Language of the agreement

The final separation agreements contained in Appendix B offer two examples of wording. The first example uses everyday nonlegalese. It was written in response to the specific request of the couple that they be able to understand clearly the entire document. The other examples in the appendix use standard legal language. I draft a memorandum of understanding covering all of the agreements reached in mediation. The couple then take this document to their lawyers for review and incorporation into the formal separation agreement. Some couples agree between themselves that they will show it to only one lawyer to save legal fees. However, I strongly recommend that each party review the agreement with his/her own attorney to be sure that his/her interests are fully protected.

To date I have not had an attorney reject the agreement—something I was afraid of when I began. At times attorneys suggest minor changes and often they contact the mediator directly to help make modifications, since the mediator understands the balance between the various parts of the agreement. One reason for lawyers accepting mediators may be that having the memorandum of understanding in hand simplifies their role and removes them from the emotional aspects of developing the agreement; another may be the fact that the clients understand what is in the agreement and how the different parts of it relate to one another. In addition, because they have owned both the process of arriving at the agreement and the content of it, they are able to explain what they intend to do, section by section.

Thus it would seem that, in the process of empowering the couple to own and control their separation agreement, the mediator also has empowered them to maintain this control after they have left mediation.

References and Useful Readings

Aspaklaria, Shelly & Geltner, Gerson. *Everything You Want to Know About Your Husband's Money . . . and Need to Know Before the Divorce*, New York: Thomas Crowell, 1979.

Auerback, Sylvia. *A Woman's Book of Money: A Guide to Financial Independence*, Garden City: Doubleday, 1976.

Bernard, Jessie. *The Future of Marriage*, New York: Bantam Books, 1972.

Biller, Henry & Meredith, Dennis. *Father Power*, Garden City: Doubleday, 1975.

Black, Melvin & Joffe, Wendy "A Lawyer/Therapist Team Approach to Divorce," *Conciliation Courts Review*. Vol. 16, No. 1, pp. 1–5, 1978.

Bohannan, Paul (Ed.). *Divorce and After: An Analysis of the Emotional and Social Problems of Divorce*, Garden City: Doubleday, 1970.

Bolles, Richard Nelson. *What Color Is Your Parachute: A Practical Manual for Job Hunters and Career Changers*, Berkeley: Ten Speed Press, 1972.

Bosco, Antoinette. *A Parent Alone*, W. Mystic, Conn.: Twenty-Third Publications, 1978.

Braudy, Susan. *Between Marriage and Divorce*, New York: New American Library, 1976.

Burden, Susan, et al. (Eds.). "The Single Parent Family." *Proceedings of the Changing Family Conference V*, Iowa City: The University of Iowa, 1976.

Cassidy, Robert. *What Every Man Should Know About Divorce*, Washington: New Republic Books, 1977.

Chapman, A. H., M.D. *Marital Brinksmanship: A Psychiatrist's Guide to Solving Marriage Problems*, New York: G.P. Putnam's Sons, 1974.

Combs, E. Raedene. "The Human Capital Concept as a Basis for Property Settlement at Divorce: Theory and Implementation," *Journal of Divorce*. Vol. 2, No. 4, pp. 329–356, 1979.

Community Council of Greater New York. *Annual Price Survey—Family Budget Costs: October 1975*, 19th ed., New York, 1976a.

———. *After Divorce: The Cost of Split Households*, Research Note No. 18, New York: May 18, 1976b.

Coogler, O. J. *Structured Mediation in Divorce Settlement*, Lexington, Mass.: Lexington Books, 1978.

Crittenden, Ann. "Nearly Half of All Fatherless Families Said to Live in Poverty," *New York Times*, p. 26, April 18, 1977.

DeMent, Sandy. "A New Bargaining Focus on Legal Services," *AFL-CIO American Federationist*. Vol. 85, No. 5, pp. 7–10, May 1978.

Deutsch, Morton. "Conflicts: Productive and Destructive," *Journal of Social Issues*. Vol. 25, No. 1, June 1969.

———. *The Resolution of Conflict*, New Haven: Yale University Press, 1973.

Elkin, Meyer. "Postdivorce Counseling in a Conciliation Court," *Journal of Divorce*. Vol. 1, No. 1, Fall 1977.

Federico, Joseph. "The Marital Termination Period of the Divorce Adjustment Process," *Journal of Divorce*. Vol. 3, No. 2, pp. 93–106, 1979.

Framo, James L. "The Friendly Divorce," *Psychology Today*. February 1978.

Franks, Maurice R. *How to Avoid Alimony*, New York: New American Library, 1975.

Frohlich, Newton. *Making the Best of It: A Common-Sense Guide to Negotiating a Divorce*, New York: Harper & Row, 1971.

Gardner, Richard A., M.D. *The Boys' and Girls' Book About Divorce*, New York: Bantam Books, 1970.

Gettleman, Susan & Markowitz, Janet. *The Courage to Divorce*, New York: Simon & Schuster, 1974.

Glick, Paul C. & Norton, Arthur J. "Marrying, Divorcing and Living Together in the U.S. Today," *Population Bulletin*. Vol. 32, No. 5, Oct. 1977.

Goldstein, J., Freud, Anna & Solnit, A. J. *Beyond the Best Interests of the Child*, New York: Free Press, 1973.

Grossman, Earl (Ed.). *Explaining Divorce to Children*, Boston: Beacon Press, 1969.

Goode, William. *After Divorce*, New York: Free Press, 1956.

Hetherington, E. Mavis, Cox, Martha & Cox, Roger. "The Aftermath of Divorce." Paper presented at the American Psychological Assn., Washington, D.C., Sept. 1976.

Hochberger, Ruth. "A New Approach to Resolve Private Quarrels," *New York Law Journal*. Vol. 177, No. 86, May 4, 1977.

Jancourtz, Isabella. *The Massachusetts Woman's Divorce Handbook*, Somerville, Mass.: New England Free Press, 1974.

Jones, Carol Adaire, Gordon, Nancy M. & Sawhill, Isabel V. "Child Support Payments in the United States," Working paper 992-03. Washington: The Urban Institute, Oct. 1976.

Kelly, Joan B. & Wallerstein, Judith. "Brief Interventions with Children in Divorcing Families," *American Journal of Orthopsychiatry*. Vol. 47 No. 1, pp. 23–39, 1977.

Kessler, Sheila. *The American Way of Divorce: Prescriptions for Change*, Chicago: Nelson-Hall, 1975.

———. *Beyond Divorce: Leader's Guide; Participant's Guide*, Atlanta: National Institute for Professional Training, 1977.

Krantzler, Mel. *Creative Divorce*, New York: Lippincott, 1974.

Laner, Mary Riege. "Love's Labor Lost: A Theory of Marital Dissolution." Doctoral dissertation, Dept. of Sociology, Virginia Polytechnic Institute and State University, 1976.

Lembeck, Ruth. *Job Ideas for Today's Woman for Profit, for Pleasure, for Personal Growth, for Esteem*, Englewood Cliffs: Prentice-Hall, 1974.

Levine, James A. *Who Will Raise the Children? New Options for Fathers (and Mothers)*, New York: Lippincott, 1976.

Lloyd, Ann. *Divorce Syndrome*, New York: Manor Books, 1977.

Maddox, Brenda. *The Half-Parent*, New York: New American Library, 1975.

Mannes, Marya & Sheresky, Norman. *Uncoupling*, New York: Viking Press, 1972.

McCormack, Patricia. "Arbitration Can Be Source of Advice for Warring Spouses,"

United Press International. Reprinted by American Arbitration Assn., Sept. 1976.

McKinney's Consolidated Laws of New York, Annotated, Book 29, Judiciary Law, McKinney, St. Paul, Minn., 1975.

Metz, Charles V. *Divorce and Custody for Men: A Guide and Primer Designed Exclusively to Help Men Win Just Settlements*, Garden City: Doubleday, 1968.

Mnookin, Robert H. & Kornhauser, Lewis. "Bargaining in the Shadow of the Law: The Case of Divorce," *Yale Law Journal*. Vol. 88, pp. 950–997, April 1979.

Montague, Louise. *A New Life Plan: A Guide for the Divorced Woman*, Garden City: Doubleday, 1978.

Morley, Ian & Stephenson, Geoffrey. *The Social Psychology of Bargaining*, London: Allen & Unwin, 1977.

Nierenberg, Gerard I. *The Art of Negotiating*, New York: Cornerstone Library, 1968.

Nuccio, Sal. *New York Times Guide to Personal Finance*, New York: Harper & Row, 1967.

Ogden, Gina & Zevin, Anne. *When a Family Needs Therapy: A Practical Assessment Guide for Parents, Lay Therapists and Professionals*, Boston: Beacon Press, 1976.

Porter, Sylvia. *Sylvia Porter's Money Book: How to Earn It, Spend It, Invest It, Borrow It and Use It to Better Your Life*, Garden City: Doubleday, 1975.

Ramos, Suzanne. *The Complete Book of Child Custody*, New York: G.P. Putnam's Sons, 1979.

Rodell, John S. *How to Avoid Alimony*, New York: Stein & Day, 1969.

Rosen, Rhona. "A Discussion of Access: Expressed Feelings of Children of Divorce Regarding Continued Contact With Non-Custodial Parent," *South African Law Journal*. Vol. 94, Part III, Aug. 1977a.

———. "The Emotional Adjustment of Children of Divorce in Relation to Sex of Custodial Parent and Interparental Turbulence." Doctoral dissertation, University of Cape Town, South Africa, 1977b.

———. "The Importance of Parent-Child Communication in the Adjustment of Children to Parental Divorce," *Psychotherapeia. Journal of the South African Institute for Psychotherapy*. Vol. 4, No. 1, 1978a.

———. "The Need for a Counselling Service for Divorcing Parents," *South African Law Journal*. Vol. 95, Part I, Feb. 1978b.

———. "A Presumption Under Scrutiny: Is There Any Real Basis for the Preference Accorded to Mothers as Custodial Parents?" *South African Law Journal*. Vol. 95, Part II, pp. 246–248, June 1978c.

Sager, Clifford J., M.D. *Marriage Contracts and Couple Therapy: Hidden Forces in Intimate Relationships*, New York: Brunner/Mazel, 1976.

Satir, Virginia, Stachowiak, James & Taschman, Harvey A. *Helping Families to Change*, New York: Jason Aronson, 1975.

Scanzoni, John. *Sexual Bargaining: Power Politics in the American Marriage*, Englewood Cliffs: Prentice-Hall, 1972.

Schoen, Robert, Greenblatt, Harry N. & Mielke, Robert B. "California's Experience with Non-Adversary Divorce," *Demography*. Vol. 12, No. 2, pp. 221–243, 1975.

Sheehy, Gail. *Passages: Predictable Crises of Adult Life*, New York: E.P. Dutton, 1976.

Sinberg, Janet. *Divorce Is a Grown Up Problem: A Book About Divorce for Young Children and Their Parents*, New York: Avon Books, 1978.

Smoke, Jim. *Growing Through Divorce*, Irvine, Cal.: Harvest House, 1976.

Spencer, Janet Maleson & Zammit, Joseph P. "Mediation–Arbitration: A Proposal for Private Resolution of Disputes Between Divorced or Separated Parents," *Duke Law Journal*. Vol. 911, 1976.

Suarez, John M., M.D., Weston, Nancy L, F.C.C. & Hartstein, Norman, M.D. "Mental Health Interventions in Divorce Proceedings," *American Journal of Orthopsychiatry*. Vol. 48, No. 2, pp. 273–282, 1978.

Thomas, Edwin J. *Marital Communication and Decision Making: Analysis, Assessment, and Change*, New York: Free Press, 1977.

Vecsey, George. "The Absent Father, Too, Can Wind Up Broke or Inside a Prison," *New York Times*, p. 26, April 18, 1977.

Wallerstein, Judith S. & Joan B. Kelly. "Divorce Counseling: A Community Service for Families in the Midst of Divorce," *American Journal of Orthopsychiatry*. Vol. 47, No. 1, pp. 4–22, 1977.

———. "The Effects of Parental Divorce: Experiences of the Child in Early Latency," *American Journal of Orthopsychiatry*. Vol. 46, No. 1, Jan. 1976a.

———. "The Effects of Parental Divorce: Experiences of the Child in Later Latency," *American Journal of Orthopsychiatry*. Vol. 46, No. 2, April 1976b.

———. "The Effects of Parental Divorce: Experiences of the Preschool Child," *Journal of the American Academy of Child Psychiatry*. Vol. 14, No. 4, Autumn 1975.

Walton, Richard E. *Interpersonal Peacemaking: Confrontations and Third Party Consultation*, Reading, Mass.: Addison-Wesley, 1968.

Weiss, Robert S. *Marital Separation*, New York: Basic Books, 1975.

Wells, Theodora. *Keeping Your Cool Under Fire: Communicating Non-Defensively*, New York: McGraw-Hill, 1980.

Wheeler, Michael. *Divided Children: A Legal Guide for Divorcing Parents*, New York: W.W. Norton, 1980.

———. *No-Fault Divorce*, Boston: Beacon Press, 1974.

Women in Transition, Inc. (Eds.). *Women in Transition: A Feminist Handbook on Separation and Divorce*, New York: Charles Scribner's Sons, 1975.

Woolley, Persia. *The Custody Handbook*, New York: Summit Books, 1979.

appendix A

Sample material given to clients entering divorce mediation

I do not have to tell you about the pain, anger, and frustration that accompany your decision to separate. I assume we are working together because you have made this decision.

Divorce mediation is a process of dissolving the marriage in a nonadversarial way. The framework provides you with the opportunity to negotiate your own settlement on the assumption that the decision to divorce has been made.

Therefore this is not an avenue to resolve conflicts of the past. You may begin to see some of those past problems in a different light, but we will not be working to resolve them. Rather we shall, through the process of mutual negotiations, attempt to define a new life with new options for both of you.

In order to do this there must develop a sense of mutual respect among the three of us. Too often divorce is placed in a win-or-lose framework. In such a case compromise is difficult, since it is seen as a loss. A smart if less than honest tactic is considered okay, because it means a win. However, the end result is a loss for both of you since winning in this situation denies a part of the other's humanity.

The divorce mediation process is designed to eliminate the win–lose atmosphere. Since the process is mutual, you cannot both win nor can you both lose. You must come out of it with a settlement that is acceptable to both of you and controlled by both of you.

And with that control comes a sense of power over the decisions affecting your lives. These are the important aspects of divorce mediation:

- nonadversarial—you are partners in the decision
- mutual—you must both agree or it does not work
- power—you control the decisions affecting your lives

When the process works you emerge from these negotiations with a new sense of dignity and a clearer sense of self and what the future holds for you. You can place the past behind you and concentrate on the future.

My function is to assist you in reaching a settlement. I do not represent either of you individually. My commitment is to a settlement you can both live with. I will use my mediation skills to help you identify the areas of agreement and the substantive areas of disagreement. Once this is done I will help you to negotiate the substantive areas of disagreement in order to reach a settlement.

As we go through the process, my role will change but always within the context of this commitment to a settlement.

In the first phase I will help you to identify the parameters for negotiations. I am available to each of you as you complete the Worksheets. I will also be working with you to define your short- and long-term goals.

Obviously, you have given this whole matter considerable thought and you have many ideas on what the ultimate settlement should include. You can use me to "sound out" ideas before actually trying them out on the other party. I can help you by sharing my experience with you of what has worked in the past and what "norms" are.

There may also be times when you want to float a trial balloon but fear what the consequences might be if it is summarily rejected. In such instances use me to "feel out" the other party. If the suggestion meets with some approval, you can then play it out in the negotiations. Using me in this way enables you to explore alternative routes to a settlement without a risk to yourself.

I cannot define the settlement and I cannot impose an agreement upon you. My role is to assist you in reaching *your* agreement. I will not take sides on any of the issues.

I am interested in the settlement as a principle and I am interested in you as people. I feel for your pain and want to help you through this difficult process and help diminish this pain. Finally, I hope to help you use these negotiations to place the past behind you. The marriage is ending, but you have a life ahead of you. That new life can be marred by holding onto the anger of the separation, or it can be an exciting opportunity to redefine yourself.

I am working for both of you to help you reach a settlement that will permit each of you to concentrate on the future and the potential it holds.

There is a typical process we will use to reach a settlement; however, your individual needs may at times cause us to depart from it. The main features of this process are as follows:

1. Develop current and future income information.
2. Develop budgets.
3. Inventory marriage assets.
4. Begin to define short- and long-term goals of each party.
5. Define general areas of agreement.
6. Define substantive areas of disagreement.
7. Identify symbolic and emotional issues.
8. Work through visitation rights and responsibilities.
9. Negotiate financial differences.
10. Develop a settlement.
11. Take the completed agreement to an attorney.

I will begin this process by meeting with you jointly. Then I will meet with you individually and move between you as necessary to work out agreements. This should lead to a long session, probably over a weekend, as we try to reach and define a final settlement.

Sessions normally last approximately one hour. However, we do not limit ourselves to sixty minutes but rather attempt to complete the business scheduled for that session.

My role as Divorce Mediator is to help you retain the power over the decision-making process that will affect your lives. My focus is on the future and helping you to define the new options open to you in your new lives.

I am not an attorney. When the final settlement is reached, you will be advised to take it to an attorney for drafting and appropriate presentation to court. I am not an accountant. As we proceed I will advise you to seek professional financial assistance on the taxation and other financial aspects of the settlement.

Typical Session Use—Each Session Is One Hour

1. Explanation of process; getting to know one and another; going over budget material.	2. Jointly working on budgets.	3. Completing budget work; beginning to establish parameters for agreement.
4. & 5. Individual meetings setting the long- and short-term goals for each party.		6. Beginning of joint bargaining by defining areas of agreement.
7. Identifying substantive areas of disagreement.	8. Working through security issues in joint and individual meetings.	9. Working through custody–visitation issues and preparing for session with the children.
10. Conducting intensive negotiations to settle other issues and arrive at settlement.	11. Holding session with the children.	12. Reviewing written agreement.

Obviously each case follows its own time frame, depending on its unique character. This model is a guide to how the process works.

Financial information

When a particular financial item seems way out of line with the general norms, I will share some averages with you. This will enable both of you to develop budgets you believe you can live with.

The financial assessment consists of three parts:

Gross income—future
Budget—past, future
Assets—past

Estimate your gross total income for the next twelve months:

	Man	Woman
Annual salary (gross)	$_____	$_____
Bonuses/commissions	_____	_____
Interest/dividends	_____	_____
Other income	_____	_____
TOTAL	_____	_____

The budget

This section deals with fixed and flexible expenses. They will differ for each party depending on certain variables. For example, which party will be primarily responsible for the child(ren)? Will one party continue to live in the present home? In most cases the party with prime responsibility for the child(ren) remains in the home. The other party, therefore, needs to calculate a budget based on an apartment rental or expense for whatever other living arrangement is planned. These expenses are best calculated on a monthly basis.

I have provided you with two sets of worksheets [reader: see pp. 165–172]. One is to be used to calculate your budget as it has been in the past twelve months: it is marked "Joint Household." The other, marked "Second Household," is for use in calculating the needs of the party moving from the present home. In addition you will find two inventory worksheets. The first, Net Worth, is designed to help you identify all the assets and liabilities of your marriage to develop a net worth. The other, Material Assets, will help you inventory your personal property and begin to think about how you might divide it [reader: see pp. 173–174].

As mentioned earlier, the prime purpose of completing this budget information is to provide you with a data base with which to make decisions. I will work on the data with you and, remember, we are looking for broad guidelines, not precise documentation. So do not be overly concerned if you cannot provide a specific figure—we will work it out together.

In many marriages one party has assumed responsibility for budgeting and handling the finances. This has left the other party "in the dark" until now. The development of these budgets will provide both parties with the same data and enable both of you, therefore, to make rational decisions concerning your futures.

Budgeting guidelines

The purpose of this budget guide is to assist you in finding out what it will cost for you to live separately. Obviously your total expenses will increase. However, in developing a budget you may also identify areas of expenditure that can be reduced without significantly changing your essential standards of living. In addition, the process of budgeting assists you in developing a rational data base from which to begin negotiations.

Budgeting is difficult for most people. Some see it as penny pinching, others as bookkeeping. Few of us like either of these activities. Yet budgeting is really financial planning that enables us to make intelligent decisions and rational choices.

Do not try to account for every dime as you prepare your past budget. Doing so will drive you to despair. Use your checkbook records as general guidelines to fill in the categories supplied here. Do not try to reconstruct every expenditure. Our purpose is to enable you to establish broad outlines, drawing on past experience, to project future needs, recognizing that your future budget will be different from the past.

There are times when the party who has had most control over the money will find it difficult to share this information. For, as you know, knowledge is often equated with power. However, if you do not share your knowledge with your spouse now when you are preparing the basis for a mutual decision, you will have to share it later with a judge who will make a unilateral decision, thereby depriving you of your power. By sharing the information now, you will both be able to keep and exercise your power.

So, in a real sense, we are working together to provide you with the power to make your own decisions about your own lives. To ensure that those decisions are mutual means sharing data at this point.

Issues raised by completing the worksheets

As you collect all the data you begin to define the parameters of an agreement. You cannot divide what you do not have. You will begin to see that living separately costs more than living together. Therefore, there must be some reduction in the standard of living of *both* parties once the separation begins.

This leads to many uncertainties and a sense of insecurity in both of you. However, the insecurity of the nonemployed party (normally the wife) responsible for custody of the children is apt to be considerably greater. That insecurity is an integral a part of these negotiations, as are the emotional issues that led to the decision to divorce. "Security" will be sitting at the negotiating table with you and you will not be able to leave until you have satisfied its needs.

The data you have prepared enable you to begin to consider some of the broad choices you need to make.

The final agreement will consist of alimony and/or child support. There are pros and cons for each of these issues and for how payments should be divided. The following table illustrates some advantages and disadvantages.

From the Viewpoint of the

	Husband	*Wife*
Alimony		
Pro	Tax deductible; automatically stops upon remarriage of ex-wife.	May provide extra money as share of tax saving; provides permanent income until remarriage.
Con	Continues forever if partner does not remarry.	Taxable item; may be a deterrant to work.
Child Support		
Pro	Provides a sense of contact with the children; ends when child(ren) are self-supporting or reach majority.	Frees you of worry about children; can give you sense of extra independence; is not taxable.
Con	Not tax deductible.	Ends when child(ren) reach majority or are self-supporting.

As you can see there are considerations that should be kept in mind—aside from the actual amounts. Each of you will probably have a different interest in these choices and the final outcome may also have an impact on the actual amount of money available. For example, if more is paid in tax deductible alimony than in child support, more aftertax dollars will be available for division.

As a previous task you calculated your gross income for next year. You will also now need to calculate your net income, for it is the net income that is available for division. When the divorce becomes final each party will file individual tax returns at the higher single taxpayer rate. In addition, there are payroll deductions that must continue and thus lower the net income—union or professional association dues will continue; pension deductions will still be made. Therefore, before we consider how much each of you will need in the future, we must first agree on how much is jointly available. That is why I have divided the Expense Worksheets into two parts, that is, Fixed and Flexible Expenses.

The net income figure will probably be adjusted as negotiations proceed. For example, if the father agrees to pay into a joint savings account a stipulated amount for the children's college education, the net figure should be reduced accordingly. You may also decide that the husband should carry some or all of the medical insurance for the children. If this is done, the net figure would also be reduced by the cost of that item.

Some couples develop an agreement whereby the husband agrees to purchase life insurance with the children as irrevocable beneficiaries. The cost of doing this also reduces the net figure.

These are some of the security issues I mentioned earlier. Since they deal with the unknown and add to the fear of the future, it may be useful to work these items out first and then move to other issues.

Any agreement that is focused on the future should include practical plans for the wife to achieve a measure of financial independence. When the wife works, her income begins to add to the available funds. But before she can work she may well need training or schooling. Therefore you should consider an arrangement that will enable the wife to go back to school (who pays tuition?) or back to work (who pays for day care?). Then, some target date should be set at which part of this income is added to the net, which would result in a reduction of the husband's share.

This needs a lot of careful thinking and discussion. The wife should be moving toward independence. However, if the reduction in alimony precisely equals the amount of new earnings, you have built in a disincentive to independence.

Now, while we are talking about additional income, we also need to consider (1) the possibility of an increase in the husband's income and (2) inflation. Depending upon where the husband is on an earnings trajectory, the wife should consider an escalation clause tied to future raises. Let us assume that the man has not reached his peak earnings level and that separation now will significantly lower everyone's standard of living. The wife may want a clause that builds in an automatic increase in alimony/child support by a specified percentage of each raise.

On the other hand, the wife may decide that the husband has reached his peak in earnings and that they will increase only through cost-of-living raises. In this case she may want to adjust the alimony/child support annually by an agreed-upon cost-of-living amount.

If you have been shopping lately for a new car or to replace furniture, you know just how expensive these items are. If you are just making ends meet and the washing machine breaks down for good, no amount of wishing will get you a new one. So think about the cars, appliances, furniture, and other high-cost items you have that might need replacement in the next two years and include them in Work Sheet II.

Considering the children

So far we have concentrated on the economic issues. But what about the kids? In our society people generally think about children in three ways:

(1) As chattel: "They *belong* to me. I've invested all I have in them. I see in them my hopes for the future."

(2) As weapons: "If he thinks he's going to see them whenever he (they?) wants, he's nuts."

"If I'm paying for them, I'm going to decide who visits with her and when I see the kids."

(3) As people: Afraid about the future, divided in loyalty, having feelings and needs independent of either of you.

Most of us have a combination of these feelings and sorting out which of the feelings are valid is difficult.

One family-court judge has developed a Bill of Rights of Children in Divorce Actions. Among these rights are:

1. To be treated as an interested and affected person and not as a pawn, possession, or chattel of either or both parents.
2. To grow to maturity in the home environment that will best guarantee an opportunity for the child to mature to responsible citizenship.
3. To receive the day-by-day love, care, discipline, and protection of the parent having custody of the child.

4. To know the noncustodial parent and to have the benefit of such parent's love and guidance through adequate visitations.
5. To have a positive and constructive relationship with both parents, with neither of them permitted to degrade or downgrade the other in the mind of the child.
6. To have moral and ethical values developed by precept and practices and to have limits set for behavior so that early in life the child may develop self-discipline and self-control.
7. To receive the most adequate level of economic support that can be provided by the best efforts of both parents.
8. To be provided with the same opportunities for education the child would have had if the family unit had not dissolved.

Obviously, neither of you wants to put the children at a disadvantage. You both want the best for them. However, if the children are viewed as bargaining tools or ignored during the negotiations, there is a danger of harming them.

For these reasons it is important to determine how the children can be involved in the decision-making process. They are entitled to some input on the issues affecting their lives. The precise nature of that input should be consonant with the traditional relationships of the family unit. You would not admit a six-year-old to the bargaining table as an equal. On the other hand you cannot expect a sixteen-year-old to accept placidly an arrangement s/he has had no role in shaping. Part of the negotiations will deal with how to involve the children in those parts that have a direct bearing on their lives.

There are many options open to you regarding your children. They include:

Joint custody. In this arrangement you would continue to live in close proximity (certainly within the same school district), with the children spending part of each week in each household, coming and going according to some comfortable arrangement.

Single custody. Here, there are three possibilities: (1) The children live with one of you and there is an "open" arrangement regarding visitation rights of the noncustody parent to the house, and of the children to the home of that parent. (2) There are specified arrangements detailing when and where the noncustody parent shall have access to the children. (3) There are no arrangements; the noncustody parent has no interest in relating to the children.

The joint custody arrangements might prove to be outside the realm of your expectations. But if you can plan to live close by and can tolerate the essentially unstructured nature of the arrangement, you should give it serious consideration. Most self-negotiated settlements fall between the option of single custody with an "open" arrangement and one with some specified arrangements.

During the divorcing process most parties feel that whatever child contact they are granting the noncustody parent is a concession. Such an attitude ties a stone around the custody-parent's neck. In addition to normal visitation rights, you should also consider your right to expect the noncustody parent to care for the children. For example, your brother is sick in another city. You want to visit him but the children need to stay at home because of school. If you have a tight, carefully specified visitation arrangement, you will not be able to ask the other parent to care for the children for a few days while you may have to be out of town.

You are both the children's parents, and while you may no longer be able to share the day-to-day responsibility of caring for the children, you can share the week-to-week responsibility.

Such an open arrangement also means that the children do not become a total burden on the freedom of the custody parent. This arrangement extends the partnership theory of marriage to the post-marriage relationship.

The Uniform Marriage and Divorce Code[1] recommends that the following points be considered in determining custody:

1. The age and sex of the child together with the interaction and interrelationship with both parents and siblings
2 The child's adjustment to home, school, and community
3. The mental and physical health of all involved

When considering the custody question you must also review the child-support aspect. Does the child have any assets? If so, what are the implications for child support? For example, if a grandparent has already provided for future college education, this item need not be covered in the settlement.

One other question you will have to consider is what child support consists of.

The immediate answer is money for food, clothing, shelter, health, and perhaps education. But how much? To what extent can you maintain

---

[1]The Uniform Marriage and Divorce Code was drafted by the National Conference of Commissioners on Uniform State Laws for adoption by the states in an attempt to achieve some uniformity among the state laws governing marriage and divorce. The states are free to adopt all or part of the Code.

the children in the style to which they are accustomed? For example, if you want your children to travel as part of their growth, you will need to add money to the child support to pay for this.

So in planning for the future, think about these points regarding your children:

1. They have rights.
2. You have rights to
    (a) frequent contact or
    (b) relief from the day-to-day burdens of child rearing.
3. They have needs.
4. You have aspirations for them.

How you work out the economic issues will have a significant impact on the life-style of your children. How you work out the child-caring issues will have a significant impact on the emotional life of your children.

If you do right by your children in these negotiations, there will also be a significant impact on your own future well-being.

The negotiations

Preparation

Preparation is the key to successful negotiations. That is why we have spent so much time preparing an adequate data base from which to start. Here are some good ground rules to follow at the start of the negotiations:

Know your case. First you should define what it is you need in the settlement. Once you have a broad idea of what you need, begin to think why you need it. Separate out each piece and develop in your own mind your reasons for it.

Review the other party's position. Having prepared your case, try to review the other party's case. What is his/her response likely to be to your proposals? What arguments is s/he likely to advance in opposition to your proposals? What things is s/he likely to advance to support these claims?

Identify the constraints. As you are thinking these points through, you will also begin to identify the external constraints that must be recognized and factored in. For example, you cannot divide more than is totally available. You cannot ask for $15,000 and figure on your partner living on $10,000 if the total income for both of you is only $20,000. Or if there is only one auto and one income producer, and the only way to get to work is by auto, this places a constraint on who gets the auto.

If you think these points through beforehand, you will not be surprised in the actual negotiations.

List your points. List the points you want to raise in each session and list your goals by priority. This will help you decide what to emphasize.

As you prepare for the negotiations, the task will often seem formidable. You will worry about not doing it correctly and many aspects of the preparation will rekindle your anger because it will probably touch on some of the reasons for the divorce.

Role of the mediator. My role at this point is to meet with each of you individually to develop your case. I do this by focusing on what is in your best interests, without regard to the other party, since the give and take must come from each of you in negotiations. When you have each prepared your positions, I bring you both together for the beginning of the negotiations.

Negotiations

I will start the discussion from areas of common agreement rather than from an obviously controversial area. Once you have secured a base of agreement on which to build, you will find that subsequent accommodations are more easily reached on disputed issues.

As you reach agreements I make a note of them and we remove those issues from the table, so to speak. That does not mean that we cannot reopen those issues at a later date; obviously, nothing is finalized until the settlement has been signed.

During all of the talks my focus is on reaching a settlement you can both live with. Therefore I will always be looking for the Yes, trying to avoid reaching a premature No—although there must be the recognition of the right of either party to say No to demands that are totally unacceptable to him or her.

Understanding that, you can see how necessary it is to make an effort to see the other's point of view without losing sight of your own position. At the same time you should be well enough prepared to explain the reasonableness or acceptability of your proposals.

It is often difficult to make a decision, and the more important the decision, the more difficult it is to reach. One way of easing the burden of making a troublesome decision is to offer a "forced choice" of two alternatives. Think about situations where you can suggest two alternatives of approximately equal value. Be careful not to offer a choice between a something and a nothing. Always remember that the goal you have set can be reached in many ways. Be open to alternative plans or routes to your goal. Try also to determine which goals can be traded for a goal of your partner. Negotiating is the art of compromising—that is, giving and taking.

When tensions are high, as they must inevitably be in a divorcing situation, it is important constantly to work at minimizing them. Thus, if you win a point in the debate or when the other party concedes an item—be gracious. Credit the other with sincerity. It will make it easier for both of you to make other compromises.

Try to maintain your own sense of dignity. Do not plead your case. You have invested as much in this marriage as your partner. Explain your position, discuss the issues, try to persuade but do not plead—you have rights too.

Another important factor of negotiating is listening. You know the other party very well. Listen closely for clues as to when and how concessions are likely. *Never talk more than necessary*. Many an agreement has been lost because one party kept on talking past the point when the other was willing to agree. Also remember that you cannot give anything away when you are listening.

Stick to the point or issues under discussion. It helps if you have listed the points you want to cover before coming to any session; keep them as the central point of the discussion.

If you are not ready to commit yourself to a given point, do not get pressured. Say you need time to think it over. I will be watching and will help you avoid reaching a premature decision.

At all times try your best to keep the discussion problem-oriented; let it not become personality-centered. If it does, I will try to reorient the discussions to the issues. If that cannot be done, we will terminate the session since a personality-centered discussion is detrimental to problem solving.

Negotiating is a systematic search for solutions that will lead to a settlement you can both be comfortable with. It requires patience and some measure of good will. Even at their most successful, these negotiations cannot solve the problems that have led to your decision to separate. However, they can help you implement this decision with less pain and with a sense of dignity and control over the process. Hopefully, it will also help you place the past behind you and help you focus on the future—a future you have helped determine rather than one defined by a settlement imposed from the outside.

Joint Household
Work Sheet I: Fixed Expenses

Household & Taxes	Past		Future
Rent or mortgage	$	$	
Federal income tax[a]			
State income tax[a]			
City income tax			
Property tax			
Telephone			
Gas/electricity			
Water			
Fuel			
Garbage pick-up			
Cable TV			
Other			
Total	$	$	
Insurance[b]			
Life	$	$	
Auto			
Health & accident			
Hospitalization			
Fire & theft			
Personal property			
Social security			
Other			
Total	$	$	
Installment Payments			
Auto	$	$	
Furniture/appliances			
Charge accounts			
Credit cards			
Personal loans			
Christmas/Chanukkah club			
Other			
Total	$	$	
Education[b]			
Tuition	$	$	
Room & board			
Books			
Other			
Total	$	$	

(continued)

Joint Household
Work Sheet I: Fixed Expenses *(continued)*

Transportation	Past	Future
Auto license plates	$	$
Vehicle sticker		
Parking		
Commuting fare(s)		
Other		
Total	$	$

Personal Allowance		
Self	$	$
Child(ren) cash		
Music lessons		
Aging parents		
Other		
Total	$	$

Memberships		
Union	$	$
Professional associations		
Clubs		
Religious		
Other		
Total	$	$

Miscellaneous		
Forthcoming major repairs	$	$
Emergency fund		
Other		
Total	$	$

Total fixed expenses	$	$

---

[a]Your federal and state taxes will increase when you file individual returns.
[b]Remember to include cost for self and child(ren) if applicable.

Joint Household
Work Sheet IA: Flexible Expenses

	Past	Future
Food		
Meals at home	$	$
Meals out (including school lunches)		
Total	$	$
Household Supplies		
Cleaning supplies	$	$
Small home items		
First aid		
Total	$	$
Household Assistance		
Babysitter	$	$
Yard care		
House cleaning		
Total	$	$
Clothing		
New clothes	$	$
Self		
Child(ren)		
Laundry	$	$
Dry cleaning		
Repairs		
Total	$	$
Equipment		
New appliances[a]	$	$
New furniture[a]		
Repairs		
Total	$	$
Home Improvement		
Maintenance	$	$
Replacement[a]		
Total	$	$
Transportation		
Gas/oil	$	$
Auto repair upkeep[a]		
Noncommuting bus/train		
Total	$	$

(continued)

Joint Household
Work Sheet IA: Flexible Expenses *(continued)*

Health *(not covered by insurance)*	Past	Future
Medical	$	$
Dental		
Drugs/medication		
Total	$	$
Personal		
Grooming aids	$	$
Barber/beauty aids		
Extra food		
Theatre/movie		
Sports		
Hobbies		
Vacation		
Newspapers		
Magazines		
Stationery/postage		
Alcohol		
Tobacco		
Home entertainment		
Other		
Total	$	$
Gifts		
Birthdays	$	$
Religious celebrations		
Total	$	$
Contributions		
Religious	$	$
Charity		
Schools/colleges		
Other		
Total	$	$
Total flexible expenses	$	$

[a]Make note of any expense with high probability in next two years.

Second Household
Work Sheet II: Fixed Expenses

Household & Taxes
Rent or mortgage $
Federal income tax[a]
State income tax[a]
City income tax
Property taxes
Telephone
Gas/electricity
Water
Fuel
Garbage pick-up
Cable TV
Other
    Total $

Insurance[b]
Life $
Auto
Health & accident
Hospitalization
Fire & theft
Personal property
Social security
Other
    Total $

Installment payments
Auto $
Furniture/appliances
Charge accounts
Credit cards
Personal loans
Christmas/Chanukkah club
Other
    Total $

Education[b]
Tuition $
Room & board
Books
Other
    Total $

(continued)

Second Household
Work Sheet II: Fixed Expenses *(continued)*

Transportation
Auto license plates $
Vehicle sticker
Parking
Commuting fare(s)
Other
    Total $

Allowances
Self $
Child(ren) cash
Music lessons
Dancing lessons
Aging parents
Other
    Total $

Memberships
Union $
Professional association
Clubs
Religious
Other
    Total $

Miscellaneous
Forthcoming major repairs $
Emergency fund
Other
    Total $

Total fixed expenses $

---

[a]Your Federal and State Taxes will increase when you file individual returns.
[b]Remember to include cost for self and child(ren) if applicable.

Second Household
Work Sheet IIA: Flexible Expenses

Food
Meals at home $
Meals out (including school lunches)
    Total $

Household Supplies
Cleaning supplies $
Small home items
First Aid
    Total $

Household Assistance
Babysitter $
Yard Care
House cleaning
    Total $

Clothing
New clothes $
  Self
  Child(ren)
Laundry
Dry cleaning
Repairs
    Total $

Equipment
New appliances[a] $
New furniture[a]
Repairs
    Total $

Home Improvement
Maintenance $
Replacement[a]
    Total $

Transportation
Gas/oil $
Auto repair/upkeep[a]
Noncommuting bus/train
    Total $

(continued)

Second Household
Work Sheet IIA: Flexible Expenses *(continued)*

Health (not covered by insurance)
Medical $
Dental
Drugs/medication
    Total $

Personal
Grooming aids $
Barber/beauty aids
Extra food
Theater/movie
Sports
Hobbies
Vacation
Newspapers
Magazines
Stationery/postage
Alcohol
Tobacco
Home entertainment
Other
    Total $

Gifts
Birthdays $
Religious celebrations
    Total $

Contributions
Religious $
Charity
Schools/colleges
Other
    Total $

Total flexible expenses $

ªMake note of any expenses with high probability in next two years.

Work Sheet III
Net Worth Statement

What You Own
Cash in checking accounts $
Cash in savings accounts
Gov't. bonds @ current value
Cash surrender value of insurance
Equity in pension
Current value of annuities
Equity in real estate
Market value of securities
   Bonds
   Stocks
   Mutual funds
   Investment trusts
Other assets
   Total $

What You Owe
Current bills outstanding $
Amount owed on installment purchases
Amount owed on personal loans
Amount due on taxes
   Federal/state
   Real estate
Other liabilities
   Total $
Total assets $
Total liabilities $
Net worth $

Property or assets owned prior to the marriage are normally excluded from this calculation as are inheritances of one party during the marriage. However, there is the question of the appreciation of these items during the marriage; if either of these situations prevail, they will need special consideration.

Work Sheet IV
Material Assets Distribution

You have accumulated many assets over the span of your marriage. As you now plan
to separate, how will you divide these assets? If you are planning to move from the
present home, what will you need to take with you? If you are the party staying,
what must you have to maintain the home? In completing this worksheet, first make
an inventory of the major items in each room and then fill in the left-hand column
with this inventory. There is no need to itemize every possession; just list those that
are important furnishings for that room. Then use this inventory and list what you
will need in your new arrangement. For example, you may list under autos two
cars, a sedan and a station wagon. Under the *needs* column, you would list what
you need, for example, wagon.

Inventory	*Needs*
Auto(s)	
Appliances	
Garden equipment	
Sports equipment	
Hobby equipment	
Books	
Records	
Pets	
House plants	
TVs	
Radios	
Paintings	
Mementos	
Furnishings:	
Bedroom 1	
Bedroom 2	
Bedroom 3	
Bedroom 4	
Living room	
Dining room	
Kitchen	
Den	
Other	

appendix B

Sample agreements

Agreement using nonlegal language

This agreement is entered into by Jean   and Jack   out of a deep
respect for each other and a shared love for our son Josh.

Although we are no longer living together, we wish to protect our
individual and joint concerns for Josh. Jean will shortly leave for Oregon. It
is agreed that she will take Josh and be responsible for him from the time
she leaves New York until on or about March 31, 1978. During that time
she will provide Jack with her location at all times so that he may be in
telephone contact and be able to communicate with his son at all times.

It is also understood that by mutual consent, Josh and/or Jean shall
return to New York for the period including the Chanukka and Christmas
holidays so that Josh can be with his father at these holidays.

On or about March 31, 1978, by mutual consent of Jean and Jack, Josh
will return to New York to live with his father for six months. During that
time Jack will be responsible for Josh and shall ensure that Josh will be
available to Jean for telephone or other form of communication that Jean
should want to use.

At the end of those six months, on or about September 30, 1978, by
mutual agreement, Josh shall return to wherever Jean is residing to live
with her for the following six months. The same conditions will prevail as in
the previous custody period.

On or about March 31, 1979, Josh shall return to wherever Jack is
residing to live for the following six months with his father. The same
conditions of the previous six months shall operate during this custody
period.

During the summer of 1979 we will review the experiences of the
previous two years and attempt to determine the living arrangement that is
best suited for Josh. At that time we will attempt to develop a workable

permanent solution that, as in this agreement, recognizes the love and concern each has for Josh.

We anticipate that Josh will enter regular grade school in September 1979. We agree that it will be in Josh's best interest to reside with one parent during the regular school year and with the other parent during the summer months once regular school begins, with holiday visitations arranged as feasible.

We recognize that in order to implement this agreement there is a need to establish a fund to pay the expenses of travel from the East to the West and vice versa. Therefore, we agree to open a joint savings account and to each pay $10 per week into the account. The account shall be opened in our joint names in trust for Josh.

The first payment shall be for the week ending Friday, August 19, 1977, with payments to continue for the life of this agreement. Funds shall be withdrawn from this account only by mutual consent of Jean and Jack for the expenses incurred in traveling under the terms of this agreement.

Therefore, if there are sufficient funds by December 1977, either Josh and/or Jean shall come East to visit with Jack for the holidays or Jack will go West for the holidays.

At the end of each custody period, funds shall be withdrawn by mutual agreement to pay the expenses incurred in getting Josh from one parent to the other.

If either Jean or Jack wishes to visit Josh at any time other than the December holidays at her/his own expense, the other parent agrees to assist in making whatever arrangements are needed locally to accommodate such a visit.

It is recognized and hoped that the expenses incurred in implementing this agreement will not exceed the payments made into the joint account and that there will be a surplus in the account at the end of the two years. Such surplus shall stay in the account in trust for Josh to be given to him on his eighteenth birthday.

We recognize that this is a temporary solution to the problem of custody, and we each agree to work toward a permanent solution that will be based on the experiences of the next two years.

_____
Jean

_____
John

Memorandum of understanding as precursor to separation agreement using formal language

We have arrived at the following agreements in the process of mediation. These agreements represent a total package, carefully balancing our mutual and individual interests. They are the agreements we wish our respective attorneys to incorporate into the Separation Agreement.

Debts. All debts have been paid. Dan carries a number of credit cards and he will continue to carry them and be solely responsible for all charges made on them.

Personal property. Most of the property will stay in the house. Dan has taken what he needs and we have agreed, to our mutual satisfaction, on the distribution of all personal property. Dan will take the 1970 Dart and the savings account at the Island Federal Savings and Loan Association, while Cindy will take the 1977 Mustang.

Real Estate. We jointly own the following properties:

1. 123 Main Street, Midtown, New York, which is the main house. We intend to rent that out for the next year.
2. Hideaway, Lake Loon, Trailways, New York, which we also will try to rent out for the next year. Each of us will move into new apartments and Cindy will manage the rentals. We will open a joint account into which we will put all of the money from the rents, and each year, after all the expenses have been paid, we will share the surplus equally. If there is a deficit we will share that equally.

Joint savings. We hold a long-term savings certificate at the Island Federal Savings and Loan Association. We want to maintain joint ownership of that certificate until it matures and then we will split the proceeds equally.

Alimony. We have agreed that there will be no alimony. Rather, all the support will be in the form of child support.

Custody. Cindy will have custody of Kriss for the next two years. At the end of the two years we will review how this has worked. We have both shared equal parental responsibility in bringing up Kriss and wish to continue to do so. To do this we wish to incorporate the attached parenting clauses into the final agreement. [1]

---

[1] These clauses are items 7–12 and 14 in the actual separation agreement.

Child support. Dan will pay Cindy $600 a month in child support. He is paid monthly and will send the $600 to Cindy within three days of his pay day. This $600 is 60 percent of Dan's net take-home pay from his teaching job (gross income, less taxes, social security, disability, medical insurance, and pension contributions). Dan will continue to pay child support equal to 60 percent of his teaching salary until Cindy earns a gross salary of $8,000 a year. When Cindy's gross income exceeds $8,000 a year, Dan's percentage of his net will be reduced as follows:

When Cindy's Gross Income Is:	Dan's Payments For Child Support Shall Be Reduced to This % of His Take-Home Pay:
$ 8,001–9,000	50%
9,001–10,000	40%
10,001–12,000	30%
12,001–14,000	20%
Equal to Dan's	10%

These payments are to continue until Kriss reaches age 21. If Kriss is unmarried and financially dependent after age 21, Dan will provide support directly to Kriss. If Cindy remarries then the child support shall be reduced to 20 percent, regardless of Cindy's income, and to 10 percent if Cindy's income equals Dan's. If, two years from now, we agree to change custody of Kriss from Cindy to Dan, then Dan will not pay any support to Cindy. Dan will continue to cover Cindy and Kriss on his medical insurance at work for as long as he is permitted by his employer.

Income taxes. Dan will claim Kriss as a dependent for federal and state tax purposes. Dan and Cindy will continue to file joint tax returns for as long as it is permitted by law. We will share in any taxes due and any refunds in the same proportion as our respective incomes declared on the tax return.

Life insurance. Dan will maintain life insurance in the amount of $75,000, naming Cindy and Kriss as beneficiaries. He will not revoke them as beneficiaries before Kriss reaches age 21, or completes four years of college. In either event, on Kriss's 22nd birthday he is free to designate any beneficiary he desires.

Savings account for Kriss. Dan and Cindy plan to use the income from the rentals to establish a savings account for Kriss, primarily for her college education. Each year we will decide how much to place into the account and we will contribute equally that amount each year.

Arbitration. Having reached this agreement through mediation, we wish to provide that if we cannot reach agreement on any significant issue regarding Kriss that we agree to submit the dispute to a third person to act as an arbitrator. We will choose the arbitrator from either John M. Haynes (our mediator) or the panel of arbitrators of the Family Dispute Panel of the American Arbitration Association of Nassau County.

Agreement using formal language[2]

AGREEMENT made this 12th day of M⸍y, 1978, by and between Cindy Smith, residing at 123 Main Street, Midtown, New York (hereinafter referred to as the "Wife" or "Cindy"), and Daniel Smith, residing at 123 First Street, Midtown, New York (hereinafter referred to as the "Husband" or "Dan").

W I T N E S S E T H

WHEREAS, the Wife and the Husband were married on August 19, 1960, in Queens County, New York, and thereafter lived together in the State of New York; and

WHEREAS, one child, namely, Kriss M. Smith (hereinafter referred to as "Kriss") was born of this marriage on October 28, 1965; and

WHEREAS, in consequence of disputes and irreconcilable differences between them, the parties have separated and are living apart;

NOW, THEREFORE, in view of their intention to live apart for the rest of their lives, and to settle their respective property rights, past, present, and future, the parties promise and agree as follows:

1. *Separation of the Parties*. The Wife and the Husband shall at all times live and continue to live separately and apart from each other and dispose of property as he or she may deem fit, free from control, restraint or interference, directly or indirectly, by the other in all respects as if each were sole and unmarried, except as herein otherwise provided.

2. *Payment of Outstanding Obligations*. All mutual household obligations of the parties have been paid, except those noted in Section 3. It is agreed that all credit cards, accounts, and obligations currently held by

---

[2]This is the full separation agreement drafted by the attorneys. It incorporates the agreements reached in mediation. Those agreements are in sections 2–18, and 25.

the Husband shall continue to be held by him and he shall be solely responsible for them.

3. *Disposition of Personal Property.* The parties have divided between them, and to their mutual satisfaction, the personal effects, household furniture and furnishings, and all other articles, tangible and intangible, of personal property which heretofore had been used by them in common, and neither party will make any claim for any such articles, which are now in the possession or in the control of the other, except that this shall not include those items that the parties have agreed, for business purposes, to continue to hold jointly as defined in Section 4. The division of personal property shall include, but not be limited to: *Husband:* 1970 Dart, savings account # , held at the Island Federal Savings & Loan Association; *Wife:* 1977 Mustang.

4. *Retention of Jointly Owned Property.* The parties agree to retain joint ownership of the property known as:

(a) 123 Main Street, Midtown, New York, such property to be rented for a minimum of one year;

(b) The summer house, known as Hideaway, Lake Loon, Trailways, New York, which shall also be rented whenever possible;

(c) The long-term savings certificate # , deposited with the Island Federal Savings and Loan Association.

Income from the above jointly held properties shall be placed in a jointly maintained checking account at the   Bank. This account shall be administered by the Wife for the purposes of receiving income from the above properties and paying expenses incurred in the management of same. The Wife shall share with the Husband all records relating to these joint properties. It is further agreed that surplus income from these properties shall be distributed equally between the parties annually on May 1 of each year. Disposal of any of these items of jointly owned property shall be jointly decided by the Husband and the Wife. If the Husband and the Wife cannot agree on the use of any such item, it shall be sold and the net proceeds divided equally between them. If net income realized from any of such items is insufficient to cover direct expenses of upkeeping, maintenance, mortgage payments, insurance, and taxes, the Husband and the Wife shall jointly and equally make up the deficit.

5. *Alimony.* Except as provided herein, the Wife shall not make any claim upon the Husband for her separate support, separate maintenance, or alimony. Likewise, the Husband will not make any claim upon the Wife for separate support, separate maintenance, or alimony.

6. *Custody.* The Wife shall have legal custody of the minor child, Kriss, which custody shall be reviewed and reconsidered by the parties within two years from the signing of this Agreement. The parties agree that

each has been, and will continue to be, an equal parent with equal rights, responsibilities, and participation in guiding the care and upbringing of Kriss during her minority.

7. *Parental Cooperation*. The Wife and the Husband agree to give support to each other in their role as parents, and to take into account the consensus of the other for the physical and emotional well-being of the child. Each shall obtain the agreement of the other, in advance, with regard to any activity of Kriss that could reasonably be expected to be of significant concern to the other.

8. *Major Decisions Affecting Kriss*. The parties agree that major decisions concerning Kriss's health, welfare, education, or upbringing shall be made by the Husband and the Wife jointly, after discussion and consultation with one another. The only exception to this provision shall be that of a life-threatening emergency.

9. *Access to Records*. Each parent shall be entitled to complete and full information from any doctor, dentist consultations, psychologists, or other specialists attending the minor child Kriss for any reason whatsoever, and to have copies of any reports given to them as parent. In addition, each parent shall be entitled to complete and full information from any teacher or school giving instruction to the minor child Kriss or to which Kriss may attend, and to have copies of any report given to them as parent.

10. *Living Arrangements*. The parties are each to provide a room for Kriss in their respective homes and Kriss shall be free to live with each of them. Kriss's primary home shall be with the Wife. The Husband shall speak to Kriss at least twice each week by telephone. On each Friday evening the Husband shall pick up Kriss at the Wife's address and Kriss shall stay with the Husband through part of the following Saturday. On the last weekend of each month, Kriss shall stay with the Husband through Sunday.

11. *Vacations and Holidays*. The parties agree that Kriss shall spend approximately half of her vacation and holiday time with each parent, and that such time shall be apportioned between the parents fairly so that each may be with Kriss on some major holidays each year and during vacation time, which corresponds with each parent's vacation.

12. *Travel*. Either party may take Kriss outside the State of New York for vacations or holidays; provided, however, that the party proposing to take Kriss on such travel shall first obtain the consent of the other. If the other does not consent, or if the parties cannot agree on the distance, place, and duration of such travel, then the issue shall be submitted to arbitration provided in Section 25 below.

13. *Financial Support of the Minor Child*. The Husband shall deliver or mail to the Wife, each month, the sum of $600 within three days of

receipt of his salary check as child support for Kriss. The $600 represents approximately 60 percent of the Husband's "net take-home pay from teaching," meaning gross salary less taxes, social security, disability, medical insurance, and pension contributions. It is agreed that for so long as the Wife has no independent gross income exceeding $8,000 per year, any increase in the Husband's teaching salary shall result in a proportionate increase in the sum paid to the Wife to maintain the 60 percent ratio. The Husband shall provide medical insurance for Kriss through his place of employment; he shall also maintain coverage for the Wife so long as is permitted by insurer.

It is further agreed that should the Wife's annual independent gross income exceed $8,000, the percentage of the Husband's net take-home pay deliverable to the Wife shall be reduced as follows:

When the Wife's Independent Gross Income Is:	Husband's Payments Shall Be Reduced to the Following Percentage of His net Take-Home Pay:
$ 8,001–9,000	50%
9,001–10,000	40%
10,001–12,000	30%
12,001–14,000	20%
Equal to husband's	10%

These payments shall continue until Kriss reaches the age of twenty-one (21), or until she marries, whichever comes first. Should Kriss remain unmarried and be financially dependent after age twenty-one (21), the Husband agrees to provide suitable financial support directly to Kriss. In the event the Wife remarries before Kriss marries or reaches twenty-one (21) years of age, financial support by the Husband shall be reduced to not more than 20 percent of the Husband's net take-home pay. If actual physical custody of Kriss is with the Husband, other than during the vacations, holidays, and usual visitation contemplated by this Agreement, no payments shall be made by the Husband to the Wife for child support during any such period(s).

Any payments voluntarily made by Dan to Cindy at any time for her support and maintenance or for the support, maintenance, and education of the minor child Kriss in excess of the sums hereinabove specified shall not alter Dan's legal obligations hereunder nor create any precedent for the future. Such excess payments shall not be construed as proof or indication of the Husband's ability to make increased payments nor of the Wife's need thereof nor of the necessity for increased payments for child support, and accordingly they shall not be used in any action or proceeding for evidentiary purpose or otherwise.

14. *Gifts to Minor Child.* The Husband and the Wife hereby agree that neither will unilaterally give a gift to the minor child having a value of more than $25.00. Gifts of greater value shall, insofar as possible, be joint gifts to the child from both parents.

15. *Dependency Exemption for Tax Purposes.* In consideration of the fact that the Husband will be paying amounts of money for the care and support of Kriss, he shall be entitled to claim her as a dependent for federal and state tax purposes.

16. *Filing Joint Tax Returns.* If the parties file joint income tax returns, they will share in the payment of taxes and refunds, if any, in proportion to their share of their taxable incomes. Each of the parties hereby indemnifies and shall hold the other harmless from any claims on account of any liability for additional taxes, interest, and/or penalties for any taxable year for which the parties have heretofore filed joint income tax returns, to the extent that any such additional taxes, interest and/or penalties are assessed in connection with his or her income exceptions or deductions, and any refunds received by either party on account of such joint returns shall be divided on the same basis. The parties further agree to execute amended tax returns, if necessary, and to cooperate in every other way in connection with such tax matters, recomputing and adjusting, if necessary, the share of joint tax to be borne by each, in accordance with the provisions herein.

17. *Life Insurance.* The Husband agrees to maintain and keep in full force and effect, insurance having a death benefit of $75,000, naming Cindy and Kriss as beneficiaries. It is the intent of Dan to carry this insurance so as to be able to meet all of the financial obligations of this Agreement in the event of his death. The obligation to maintain this insurance shall cease at the point Kriss reaches the age of twenty-one (21) years or the completion of four continuous academic years of college education, whichever last occurs; but in no event past Kriss' twenty-second (22nd) birthday. At that time, Dan may designate any beneficiary of such insurance as he shall desire.

The Husband shall deliver to the Wife such insurance policies or a certificate or other instrument evidencing such designation of the Wife and Child as the beneficiaries of such insurance and the Husband shall execute and deliver all forms or documents which may be required and which may be appropriate, so that the Child and Wife shall be such beneficiaries to the extent hereinbefore set forth.

Except in order to pay premiums thereon, the Husband shall not borrow against said policy or policies, or pledge or hypothecate them in any way.

The Husband agrees and undertakes to pay, or cause to be paid, all premiums, dues, and assessments on said insurance policy or policies at least fifteen (15) days prior to the expiration of the date thereof. The Husband agrees to transmit to the Wife, upon written request by her, receipts showing that such premiums, dues, and assessments have been paid.

Any dividends on said policy or policies shall belong exclusively to the Husband and he shall be entitled either to receive said dividends or to use the same in reduction of premiums.

The Husband hereby authorizes the Wife to be informed by the insurance company or companies with respect to the status of said policy or policies and the payment of said premiums, dues, and assessments, and shall execute and deliver to the Wife such forms, instruments and documents as may be required so that the Wife may obtain such information from the insurance company or companies.

In the event of the Husband's failure to pay any of the premiums, dues, or assessments that may become due on said policy or policies within fifteen (15) days prior to the expiration of the grace dates thereof, he shall immediately become indebted to the Wife in the amount of such premiums, dues, or assessments, whether or not the same shall have been paid or advanced by the Wife. In the event that any of said policies shall have lapsed or expired, the Husband agrees that he shall immediately become indebted to the Wife in the amount of the initial premium of a new policy or policies covering the life of the Husband in the amount of the policy or policies that shall have lapsed or expired, and the Husband's obligation to continue to pay the premiums on a new policy shall continue as hereinbefore provided.

The foregoing shall not be deemed to limit in any way the rights and remedies of the Wife in the event that the Husband shall fail to perform the obligations required to be performed by him under this Article or shall fail to pay any of the premiums, dues, or assessments that may become due on said policy or policies within fifteen (15) days prior to the grace dates thereof.

Nothing herein contained shall be construed to prohibit the Husband from obtaining term life insurance.

Any payments made to the Wife pursuant to this Article must be used solely for the purpose of paying the insurance premiums due and owing on the policies in question.

18. *Savings Account*. By September 1978, the parties shall establish an interest-bearing account at a duly chartered savings bank or credit union which is insured by the Federal Deposit Insurance Corporation in their joint names as Trustees for Kriss. The Husband and the Wife, by joint agreement, shall determine the amount of money to be deposited into the account prior to September 1, 1978. On September 1, 1978, and on each succeeding September 1, the Husband and the Wife shall determine the amount which shall be deposited into the account. In deciding the amount the parents shall primarily consider the welfare of the child. Though the major purpose of this account shall be the expense of future education, the parties may agree to use portions of the fund for other major fixed expenses or for travel for Kriss. The obligation to contribute to the account shall terminate when Kriss reaches twenty-one (21) years of age.

19. *Release by the Parties*. Subject to the provisions of this Agreement, each party has remised, released, and forever discharged, and by these presents does for himself or herself, and his or her heirs, legal representatives, executors, administrators, and assigns, remise, release, and forever discharge the other of and from all cause or causes of action, claims, rights, or demands whatsoever in law or in equity which either of the parties hereto ever had or now has against the other, except any and all cause or causes of action for divorce.

20. *Waiver by the Parties*. Each of the parties hereto, each for himself and herself, respectively, and for their respective heirs, legal representatives, executors, administrators, and assigns, hereby waives any right of election that he or she may have or hereafter acquire regarding the estate of the other, or to take against any last Will and Testament of the other, whether heretofore or hereafter executed, as provided for in any law, now or hereafter effective, of the State of New York or any other state or territory of the United States, or any foreign country, and renounces and releases all interest, right, or claim of distributive share or intestate succession or dower or curtesy or otherwise that he or she now has or might otherwise have against the other or the estate of the other, or the property of whatsoever nature, real or personal, of the other, under or by virtue of the laws of any state or country, and each will, at the request of the other, or his or her legal representatives, executors, administrators, and assigns, execute, acknowledge, and deliver any and all deeds, releases, or other instruments necessary to bar, release, or extinguish such interests, rights, and claims, which may be needful for the proper execution of any provisions of this Agreement.

The parties have agreed that, for so long as either is unmarried, the other shall be the executor of each party's will. Upon the remarriage of either party, each of the parties renounces and relinquishes any and all claims and rights that he or she may have or may hereafter acquire to act as executor or administrator of the other party's estate.

21. *Rights of the Parties*. Nothing herein contained shall be construed to prevent either of the parties from instituting an action for absolute divorce against the other. In the event that a temporary interlocutory, or final judgment, order, or decree of divorce is rendered in any proceeding between the parties hereto, the terms of this Agreement shall not be questioned by the parties hereto in any such proceeding, but shall continue to bind the parties, and, if incorporated in any such decree, shall be deemed to survive such decree and not become merged therein.

22. *Totality of the Agreement*. Both parties acknowledge that no representations of any kind have been made to him or her as an instrument to enter into this Agreement other than the representations set forth herein, and that this Agreement contains all the terms of the contract and constitutes the entire understanding between the parties.

23. *Modification of the Agreement*. This Agreement shall not be modified or annulled by the parties, except by written instrument executed in the same manner as this instrument. The failure of either party to insist upon the strict performance of any provision of this Agreement shall not be deemed a waiver of the rights to insist upon a strict performance of such provision or of any other provision of this Agreement at any time.

24. *Understanding of the Agreement*. Both the legal and practical effect of this Agreement in each and every respect and the financial status of the parties has been duly explained to both parties and they both acknowledge that it is a fair agreement which represents the entire understanding of the parties. There are no representations, promises, warranties, covenants, or undertakings other than those expressely set forth herein.

25. *Arbitration*. In the event that agreement cannot be reached regarding some significant aspect of the care and custody of the minor children, and after diligent effort by the parties to resolve such dispute between themselves, the parties agree to submit their dispute to a third person to act as an arbitrator. Such third person may be chosen from among a panel maintained by:

The American Arbitration Association in the County of Nassau,

or

John M. Haynes, Northport, New York

26. If any provision of this Agreement is held to be invalid or unenforceable, all other provisions shall nevertheless continue in full force and effect.

27. The Husband and the Wife agree to share equally all legal costs in connection with this separation.

IN WITNESS WHEREOF, the parties hereto have set their hands and seals the day and year first above written.

_____

Cindy Smith

_____

Daniel Smith

STATE OF NEW YORK)
                   : ss.:
COUNTY OF NASSAU)

On this   day of   , 1978, before me personally came CINDY SMITH to me personally known to be the same person described in and who executed the foregoing instrument and acknowledged that she executed the same.

_____

STATE OF NEW YORK)
                   : ss.:
COUNTY OF NASSAU)

On this   day of   , 1978, before me personally came DANIEL SMITH to me personally known to be the same person described in and who executed the foregoing instrument and acknowledged that he executed the same.

_____

MEMORANDUM
OF
SEPARATION AGREEMENT

The undersigned, CINDY SMITH, residing at 123 Main Street, Midtown, New York, ('Wife") and DANIEL SMITH, residing at 123 First

Street, Midtown, New York ("Husband"), do hereby acknowledge that we we were married to each other on August 19, 1960; that subsequently we entered into an agreement of separation dated May 12, 1978, which was subscribed and acknowledged by us on May 12, 1978.

_____

Cindy Smith

_____

Daniel Smith

STATE OF NEW YORK)

                : ss.:

COUNTY OF NASSAU   )

    On this   day of   , 1978, before me personally came CINDY SMITH to me personally known to be the same person described in and who executed the foregoing instrument and acknowledged that she executed the same.

_____

STATE OF NEW YORK)

                : ss.:

COUNTY OF NASSAU   )

    On this   day of   , 1978, before me personally came DANIEL SMITH to me personally known to be the same person described in and who executed the foregoing instrument and acknowledged that he executed the same.

_____

Sample clauses from Ben and Bea's agreement that differ from Cindy and Dan's

Ben and Bea's "Retention of Jointly Owned Property" provided for a way of disposing of it and sharing the proceeds:

Retention of Jointly Owned Property. The parties agree to retain joint ownership of the property known as   ,   , New York. The Husband shall continue to reside at such house. On or before July 1, 1980, this property shall be sold at fair market price and the proceeds (being the sum left after the mortgage debt, real estate broker's fee, attorney's fee, and the $3,000 loan to   have all been paid) shall be evenly divided between the Wife and Husband. No later than January 15, 1980, the parties shall select a real estate appraiser to establish a fair market value for the house. Either may have the option to purchase the property at that price or the property shall be placed on the market for sale by February 15, 1980, with a closing date of no later than July 1, 1980. The fee, if any, for the appraisal shall be shared equally.

Should the Husband choose to rent out part of the property while he resides there, the income from such rental shall be shared equally. The Husband shall collect the rent monthly and convey the Wife's share to her by the fifteenth (15th) day of each month.

Their child support agreement was also different:

Financial Support of the Minor Children. Any financial support required for Sam shall be met by the Husband. The Husband shall pay to the Wife, each week, the sum of $100 to be paid each Friday, being child support for Alice. The Husband shall provide medical-dental insurance for the children with benefits no less than currently enjoyed, for all times that the Husband is employed, regardless of the conditions of employment. All child-support payments to the Wife shall cease after the February 1, 1980, payment. In the event Alice opts to live with the Husband, these child-support payments shall cease. In the event Alice chooses to live with the Husband for more than one month, child-support payments to the Wife shall not be made for as long as Alice lives with the Husband. Child-support payments shall also cease if Alice is emancipated, married, joins the military, or is deceased. The Husband shall also pay all tuition for Alice for at least two years commencing with the Spring 1980 semester. Tuition costs shall be limited to a state college or university or, in the event Alice attends private college he shall pay tuition up to the amount then charged by   College, Long Island, New York. (This college has the average private tuition rate.)

The life insurance clause protected the children of this marriage as follows:

Life Insurance and Other Death Benefits for Minors. Both parties agree to amend the life insurance policies held by them to show the children, Alice and Sam, as co-beneficiaries of the proceeds. In the case of the Husband this shall apply to the $10,000 policy held individually, the life insurance in effect through his place of employment, and any death benefits that may accrue from a pension plan. In the case of the Wife this shall apply to the $5,000 policy held individually.

In addition, both parties agree to draw up wills within three months from the signing of this agreement declaring the children, Alice and Sam, as sole beneficiaries of their respective estates. In the event either party remarries that party agrees to provide that the children of this marriage, Alice and Sam, shall not receive less than 50 percent of the estate.

They needed special protection on the co-signed loan:

> *Protection Against Default of a Loan.* The Husband is the co-signator of a loan, originally in the amount of $5,000, which was used by the Wife for business purposes. The Wife agrees that, should she default on that loan and the Husband be held liable for the balance, the Husband shall be repaid said amount from the Wife's share of the equity in the property at   ,   , New York.

Bea's interest in Ben's social security was protected by this paragraph:

> *Understanding Regarding Conversion.* In recognition of the provision of the Social Security Act regarding widows' benefits, the Husband agrees not to seek to convert this Separation Agreement into a permanent divorce decree before July 3, 1980.

Index